Mike McGrath

Fortran
Programming

in easy steps

In easy steps is an imprint of In Easy Steps Limited
16 Hamilton Terrace · Holly Walk · Leamington Spa
Warwickshire · United Kingdom · CV32 4LY
www.ineasysteps.com

Notice of Liability
Every effort has been made to ensure that this book contains accurate
and current information. However, In Easy Steps Limited and the
author shall not be liable for any loss or damage suffered by readers
as a result of any information contained herein.

Trademarks
All trademarks are acknowledged as belonging to their respective
companies.

In Easy Steps Limited supports The Forest Stewardship Council (FSC),
the leading international forest certification organization. All our titles
that are printed on Greenpeace approved FSC certified paper carry the
FSC logo.

MIX
Paper from
responsible sources
FSC® C020837

Printed and bound in the United Kingdom

ISBN 9781787910355

Contents

9   Programming objects   139

10   Threading apps   153

11   Analyzing data   171

Index   187

How to use this book

The examples in this book demonstrate features of the Fortran programming language, and the screenshots illustrate the actual results produced by executing the listed code examples.

Certain colorization conventions are used to clarify the code listed in the steps – these are the same colors used by default in Microsoft Visual Studio to colorize Fortran code:

- General program code and numeric values are colored black.

- Fortran keywords and intrinsic function names are colored blue.

- Literal character strings are red.

- Code comments are green.

For example...

```fortran
program main
    implicit none
    ! Display the traditional greeting.
    print *, achar(10), 'Hello, World!'
end program
```

To easily identify the source code for the example programs described in the steps, a file icon and file name appears in the margin alongside the steps:

hello.f90

Grabbing the source code

For convenience I have placed source code files from the examples featured in this book into a single ZIP archive. You can obtain the complete archive by following these easy steps:

1 Visit **www.ineasysteps.com** and log in, then navigate to Free Resources and click the Browse Now button in the Source code downloads and other book resources section

2 Find Fortran Programming in easy steps in the list, then click on the hyperlink entitled All code examples to download the archive

3 Now, extract the archive contents to any convenient location on your computer

The screenshots in this book illustrate the actual results of executing the listed code steps. If you don't achieve the result illustrated in any example, simply compare your code to that in the original example files you have downloaded to discover where you went wrong.

1 Getting started

Welcome to the exciting world of Fortran programming. This chapter introduces Fortran, and describes how to set up the Fortran environment and how to create Fortran programs.

Introducing Fortran

The Fortran (Formula Translation) computer programming language revolutionized programming when it was first introduced in 1957 by John Backus and his team at IBM.

Previously, program instructions were written in Assembly language machine code, which was tedious, time consuming, and prone to errors. Fortran allowed programmers – for the first time – to write instructions in human-readable form, which could then be automatically translated into machine code by a "compiler".

Fortran greatly reduced the time needed to create computer programs, so was enthusiastically received, especially by scientists who could now develop high-level scientific applications. Universities and research institutions quickly adopted Fortran.

Although originating many years ago, Fortran has since been frequently updated to introduce new programming features:

- **Fortran II (1958)** – added **function** and **subroutine** structures, allowing reusable blocks of code.

- **Fortran IV (1962)** – added conditional **if** test statements and established distinct data types.

- **Fortran 77 (1978)** – added conditional **if else** test statements and **character** string handling capabilities.

- **Fortran 90 (1991)** – added support for **array**, **module**, and **recursive** structures.

- **Fortran 2003** – added support for the Object Oriented Programming (OOP) paradigm.

- **Fortran 2008** – added support for **coarray** structures to enable parallel programming.

More recently, **Fortran 2018** saw a significant revision, and a minor extension in **Fortran 2023** ensures that Fortran continues to meet the demands of modern computing.

Throughout the years, the concepts introduced by Fortran have influenced the development of other programming languages such as C, Python, and Java. The emphasis in Fortran is firmly placed on efficient computation and speed of execution, which makes it attractive for use in processing large numeric datasets.

Advantages of Fortran

- Exceptional array processing capabilities.

- Fast numerical computation.

- Minimal runtime overhead cost.

- Stable, mature language with extensive libraries.

- Backward compatibility with older Fortran code.

- Compiler optimizations for speed.

- Strong support for parallel computing.

- Portable across different platforms.

- Efficient handling of large datasets.

- Interoperable with other programming languages.

- Support for off-loading computations from Central Processor Units (CPU) to Graphic Processor Units (GPU).

- Enhanced vectorization capabilities to take advantage of modern CPU architectures.

Fortran in action

Fortran's efficiency and its ability to process complex numerical computations means it can perform a pivotal role in High Performance Computing (HPC). The support for parallel computing is crucial for HPC applications. Fortran is, therefore, widely used in supercomputing applications, such as:

- Finite element analysis.

- Forecasting models.

- Fluid dynamics.

- Astrophysics simulations.

- Weather prediction.

The renewed popularity of Fortran is due to its unmatched performance and ongoing modernization. These ensure Fortran will remain a valuable computer programming asset.

Installing compilers

Fortran programs can be created in any plain text editor, such as Windows' Notepad app, but in order to create executable applications from Fortran code, it is necessary to install a Fortran compiler on your computer.

There are several free Fortran compilers available, offering varying degrees of support for the various Fortran standards. The most standards-compliant, however, are the two free Fortran compilers offered by Intel, which integrate with Microsoft Visual Studio:

- **Intel Fortran Compiler Classic (ifort)** – supports most language standards and is available for Windows, Linux, and macOS operating systems.

- **Intel Fortran Compiler (ifx)** – fully supports all language standards including the Fortran 2018 standard and some features of Fortran 2023.

The Intel Fortran Compiler (ifx) is the most modern compiler and is available for the Windows operating system as part of Intel's **oneAPI HPC Toolkit**. The open standard "oneAPI" adopted by Intel is a unified Application Programming Interface (API) for use across different computer architectures.

Before installation of the **oneAPI HPC Toolkit** containing the Fortran ifx compiler, you must first install Intel's **oneAPI Base Toolkit**, which provides a core set of tools and libraries.

1 Browse to **intel.com** and search for **oneAPI Base Toolkit download**, then select the Operating System option for **Windows** and click the **Online Installer** button

The Intel oneAPI Toolkits require systems based on certain x64 Intel CPUs and specific GPUs. Refer to the System Requirements for each oneAPI Toolkit on the Intel website.

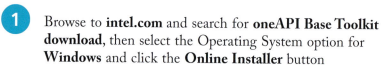

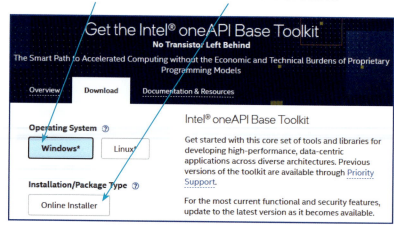

Get the Intel® oneAPI Base Toolkit

No Transistor Left Behind

The Smart Path to Accelerated Computing without the Economic and Technical Burdens of Proprietary Programming Models

Overview   Download   Documentation & Resources

Intel® oneAPI Base Toolkit

Operating System ⓘ

Windows*   Linux*

Get started with this core set of tools and libraries for developing high-performance, data-centric applications across diverse architectures. Previous versions of the toolkit are available through Priority Support.

Installation/Package Type ⓘ

Online Installer

For the most current functional and security features, update to the latest version as it becomes available.

...cont'd

2 On the next page, enter your email address and country, then click the **Submit & Begin Download** button

3 Follow the "Installation Instructions for Windows" steps to complete installation of the **oneAPI Base Toolkit**

4 Now, search at **intel.com** for **oneAPI HPC Toolkit download**, then repeat the installation procedure to install that toolkit – which contains both Intel Fortran compilers

The oneAPI HPC Toolkit is designed to integrate with Microsoft Visual Studio, so this must be installed on your system along with its Desktop developer tools for C++ component. The free Community Edition of Visual Studio can be downloaded from visualstudio.microsoft. com/downloads

5 When installation has completed, there will be a new Intel group added to your Start menu Apps list

6 Select the **Intel oneAPI command prompt for Intel 64** item to initialize the oneAPI environment

7 Enter **ifx /QV** at the command prompt to confirm installation of the Intel Fortran ifx compiler

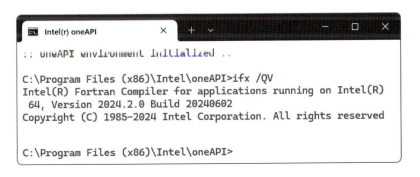

Writing programs

Fortran programs can be written in any plain text editor, such as Windows' Notepad app (or in Visual Studio's code editor), but must adhere to one of two formats:

- **Fixed-form** – limited to 72 columns where the first six columns serve special purposes. For example, an **&** ampersand in column 6 indicates a line continuation. Program files in this format are typically saved with a **.f** file extension.

- **Free-form** – can use 132 columns with no special columns. Line continuation is indicated by an **&** ampersand at the end of a line. Program files in this format are typically saved with a **.f90** file extension.

The fixed-form format was superseded by the free-form format upon the release of the Fortran 90 standard, and has become the preferred format for Fortran program files.

Each Fortran program is a block of code that begins with the **program** keyword, followed by an identifier name chosen by the programmer – typically the name "main". The program block contains a specification section followed by an executable section and ends with the **end program** keywords. The specification section should always contain the **implicit none** keywords to ensure explicit declaration of "variables" in the code. So the syntax of a Fortran program block looks like this:

Fortran needs to know the type of data each variable can contain in a program. The **implicit none** statement enforces this rule so that the type cannot be implied "on-the-fly" as in some other programming languages.

12

```
                    program main
......................................
Specification section          implicit none
......................................

Executable section

......................................
                    end program
```

Specification section

Executable section

It is good practice to indent code within the program block for clarity. Additionally, explanatory comments can be included within the code by prefixing the comment by an **!** exclamation character – any line that begins with an **!** is ignored by the compiler.

Fortran provides no means to include multi-line comments.

1 Open a plain text editor and begin a Fortran program by creating a program block

program main

end program

hello.f90

2 Next, insert the required statement within the program block's specification section

implicit none

3 Now, insert a comment and a statement within the program block's executable section to output a message

! Output a new line and the traditional greeting.

print *, achar(10), 'Hello, World!'

Hot tip

The **print *** statement sends "list-directed" output to the screen. The **achar(10)**, statement sends the ASCII code character 10 (a newline) to the screen – this can alternatively be achieved with **new_line('C')**.

4 Save the file named as **hello.f90** in a convenient location – for example, in a "MyPrograms" folder at **C:\MyPrograms**

5 To create an executable version of the program, first initialize the oneAPI environment, as explained on page 11

6 Then, at the command prompt, navigate to the location of the program file – for example

cd C:\MyPrograms

7 Enter this command to compile the program and create an executable file named "hello"

ifx hello.f90

Hot tip

The compiler command first creates an object file then an executable file.

8 Finally, enter the executable file name to run the program and see the greeting output

hello

```
C:\MyPrograms>hello

Hello, World!

C:\MyPrograms>
```

13

Creating variables

A "variable" is like a container in a Fortran program, in which a data value can be stored inside the computer's memory. The stored value can be referenced using the variable's name.

The programmer can choose any name for a variable, providing it adheres to the Fortran naming conventions – a chosen name may only contain letters, digits, and the underscore character, but must begin with a letter. Also, Fortran keywords – like those listed on the inside cover of this book – must be avoided. It's good practice to choose meaningful names to make the code more comprehensible.

To create a new variable in a program it must be "declared" in the program's specification section, specifying the type of data it may contain and its chosen name – using this syntax:

> *data-type* :: *variable-name*

Multiple variables of the same data type can be created in a single declaration as a comma-separated list with this syntax:

> *data-type* :: *variable-name1, variable-name2, variable-name3*

The five basic Fortran data types are listed in the table below, together with a brief description and example content:

Data Type	Description	Example
integer	An integer whole number	100
real	A floating-point number	3.1415
complex	Two consecutive floating-point numbers	2.5, 4.0
character	A single byte, capable of holding one character	'A'
logical	A Boolean value of true or false. Numerically, zero is false and negative one is true	.false. or 0 .true. or -1

Fortran is not case sensitive but names should be in lowercase and preferably short. Where longer names are required, the underscore character can be used – for example, **shape_class**.

Hot tip

Character values of the **character** data type can be enclosed between a pair of single quotes or a pair of double quotes. Single quotes are used in the examples in this book.

1 Begin a Fortran program by creating a program block

```fortran
program main


end program
```

vars.f90

2 Next, insert the required statement and declare some variables within the program block's specification section

```fortran
implicit none
integer :: inum
real :: rnum
complex :: cnum
logical :: bool
character(len=16) :: str        ! A 16-character string.
```

Notice how **(len=16)** is used here to specify that this **character** data type variable can contain up to 16 characters.

3 Now, insert statements within the program block's executable section to initialize the variables with values

```fortran
inum = 127
rnum = 98.6
cnum = (16,32)
bool = .true.
str = 'Fortran Coding'
```

4 Then, add statements to output the variable values

```fortran
print *, achar(10), ' Number:', inum
print *, 'Decimal:', rnum
print *, 'Complex:', cnum
print *, 'Status:', bool
print *, 'String:', str
```

Different values can be assigned to any variable as the program proceeds, so their value can vary – hence the term "variable".

5 Save the file named as **vars.f90**, then compile and run the program to see the variables' initial values

```
ifx vars.f90
vars
```

15

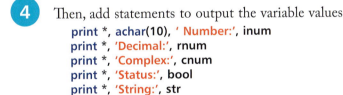

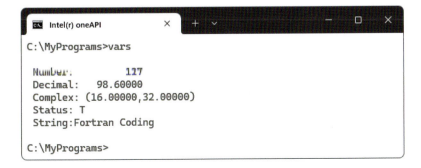

```
Intel(r) oneAPI              ×    + ∨          —   □   ×

C:\MyPrograms>vars

 Number:            127
 Decimal:   98.60000
 Complex: (16.00000,32.00000)
 Status: T
 String:Fortran Coding

C:\MyPrograms>
```

Creating constants

Data that will not change during the execution of a program should be stored in a constant container, rather than in a variable. This better enables the compiler to check the code for errors – if the program attempts to change the value stored in a constant, the compiler will report an error and compilation will fail.

A constant can be created for any data type by including a **parameter** keyword in the declaration. Unlike variables, constants must always be initialized in the declaration with this syntax:

> *data-type*, **parameter** :: *constant-name = value*

Typically, constant names appear in uppercase to distinguish them from (lowercase) variable names.

1000000

const.f90

1 Begin a Fortran program by creating a program block
program main

end program

2 Next, insert the required statement and declare a constant plus two variables within the specification section
implicit none
real, parameter :: PI = 3.1415927
real :: dia, rim

3 Now, insert statements within the program block's executable section to perform multiplication and to output the result
dia = 5.0
rim = PI * dia
print *, achar(10), ' Diameter:', dia, 'Circumference:', rim

4 Save the file named as **const.f90**, then compile and run the program to see the variables' values
ifx const.f90

Hot tip

Add a statement to assign a new value to the constant, then try to compile the program to see it fail.

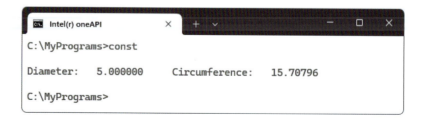

```
Intel(r) oneAPI                    ×   +  ∨              —   □   ×

C:\MyPrograms>const

Diameter:    5.000000    Circumference:    15.70796

C:\MyPrograms>
```

Choosing sizes

Declarations of the **integer** and **real** data types can specify the maximum size of number they may contain to a **kind** specifier.

> *data-type*(kind= *n*) :: *variable-name*

The value assigned to the **kind** specifier dictates how many bytes of storage space it will be allocated. Possible **integer** values are 1, 2, 4, or 8, and possible **real** values are 4 ("single precision"), 8 ("double precision"), or 16 ("quadruple precision"). Stating the variable name in the parentheses of the intrinsic **huge()** function, as its "argument", reveals its maximum possible numeric value.

1 Begin a Fortran program by creating a program block

```
program main

end program
```

2 Next, insert the required statement and declare variables of different size within the specification section

```
implicit none
integer(kind=1) :: small_int
integer(kind=2) :: medium_int
integer(kind=4) :: large_int
integer(kind=8) :: very_large_int
```

3 Now, insert statements in the program block's executable section to reveal each variable's possible maximum

```
print *, achar(10), ' Small:', huge(small_int)
print *, 'Medium:', huge(medium_int)
print *, 'Large:', huge(large_int)
print *, 'Very Large:', huge(very_large_int)
```

4 Save the file named as **size.f90**, then compile and run the program to see the variables' maximum values

```
ifx size.f90
```

```
C:\MyPrograms>size

 Small:  127
 Medium:  32767
 Large:  2147483647
 Very Large:   9223372036854775807

C:\MyPrograms>
```

size.f90

Hot tip

If no **kind** value is specified, the default size for both **real** and **integer** data types is four bytes (32-bit numbers).

Hot tip

When used without an **achar(10)** newline character, the **print** statement leaves a space before the output. Historically, the first column was used for old line-printer control characters.

Creating pointers

A pointer variable points to an area of dynamically allocated memory and is created by a **pointer** keyword in its declaration.

> **data-type, pointer :: *variable-name***

Memory space must be provided by stating the pointer variable's name as the argument to an intrinsic **allocate()** function, and when that space is no longer needed it can be freed in a similar way by an intrinsic **deallocate()** function.

The memory location address of a variable can be revealed by stating its name as the argument to an intrinsic **loc()** function.

F

ptr.f90

1 Begin a Fortran program by creating a program block
```
program main
    implicit none
```

2 Declare two variables and allocate pointer memory space
```
    integer(kind=1) :: num
    integer(kind=1), pointer :: ptr
    allocate(ptr)
```

3 Now, insert statements within the program block's executable section to initialize the variables
```
    num = 10
    ptr = num
```

4 Output the value and location of each variable, then free the memory space allocated for the pointer
```
    print *, achar(10), ' Integer:', num, 'at:', loc(num)
    print *, 'Pointer:',  ptr ,'at:', loc(ptr)
    deallocate(ptr)
end program
```

5 Save the file named as **ptr.f90**, then compile and run the program to see the variables' values and location

Beware

Here, the pointer variable is assigned the value of the regular integer variable assigned to it at the time of the assignation. The value of the pointer variable will not automatically change if the integer variable is subsequently assigned a new value.

```
Intel(r) oneAPI                    ×    +  ∨         —  □  ×

C:\MyPrograms>ptr

Integer:    10 at:        641717107319
Pointer:    10 at:       2612263988192

C:\MyPrograms>
```

18

Linking targets

A target variable can be associated with a pointer variable, and is created by including a **target** keyword in its declaration.

> *data-type*, target :: *variable-name*

The association is made by assigning the target variable to the pointer variable using the Fortran **=>** association operator. This link can be broken by stating the pointer variable name as the argument to an intrinsic **nullify()** function.

1 Begin a Fortran program by creating a program block
```
program main
    implicit none
```

2 Declare two variables and create an association
```
integer(kind=1), pointer :: ptr
integer(kind=1), target :: tgt
ptr => tgt
```

3 Next, insert statements within the program block's executable section to initialize the target variable and output the value of both variables
```
tgt = 8
print *, achar(10), 'Pointer:', ptr, 'Target:', tgt
```

4 Next, add statements to change the target variable's value, output the value of both variables, then break the link
```
tgt = 4
print *, achar(10), 'Pointer:', ptr, 'Target:', tgt
nullify(ptr)
end program
```

5 Save the file named as **tgt.f90**, then compile and run the program to see that the variables' values are linked

tgt.f90

When a pointer is associated with a target, the value of the pointer changes when the target's value changes. Likewise, the value of the target changes when the pointer's value changes.

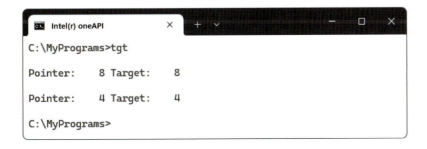

```
Intel(r) oneAPI

C:\MyPrograms>tgt

Pointer:    8 Target:    8

Pointer:    4 Target:    4

C:\MyPrograms>
```

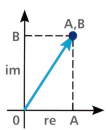

Getting complex

The **complex** data type is used to store a complex number consisting of two parts, each part being a floating point number. The first number is the "real" (**re**) part and the second number is the "imaginary" (**im**) part.

The complex number can be represented visually as a "complex plane" in an Argand diagram. For example, the complex number **(3.0, 4.0)** is plotted by three units along the horizontal real axis and by four units along the vertical imaginary axis. The point where the two intersect on the complex plane represents the complex number.

In Fortran, each part of a complex number is considered to be a "member" of that object. These can be referenced using the Fortran **%** member operator after the variable name, followed by **re** (for the first part) or followed by **im** (for the second part).

Complex numbers are used for mathematical calculation in many fields, such as engineering, physics, and signal processing. One simple use is to implement the Pythagoras theorem by having the intrinsic **abs()** function return the absolute value of its argument.

comp.f90

1 Begin a Fortran program that declares a complex constant

```fortran
program main
    implicit none
    complex, parameter :: COMP = (3,4)
```

2 Output the value of each part and the absolute value

```fortran
    print *, achar(10), ' Side A Length:', COMP%re
    print *, 'Side B Length:', COMP%im
    print *, 'Hypotenuse C :', abs(COMP)
end program
```

3 Save the file named as **comp.f90**, then compile and run the program to see the complex number values

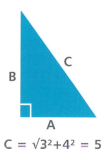

$C = \sqrt{3^2+4^2} = 5$

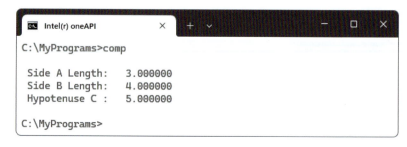

Creating types

In addition to the five basic data types, Fortran allows the programmer to create derived data types. These are structures that can contain several data objects of various data types. The structure begins with the **type** keyword and a chosen name, and is terminated by **end type** keywords – so its syntax looks like this:

```
type type-name
    declarations
end type
```

Each data object declared in a derived type structure is a "member" of that derived data type. This means they can be referenced using the Fortran **%** member operator after the type name, followed by the data object's name. Derived data types can be used to represent a record, such as details of a book.

1   Begin a Fortran program that defines a derived type
```
program main
    implicit none
    type Book
        character(len=16) :: title, author
        integer(kind=8) :: num
    end type
```

derive.f90

2   Create an "instance" of the derived type and assign values to its members
```
type(Book) :: c_book
c_book%title = 'C Programming'
c_book%author = 'Mike McGrath'
c_book%num = 788457
```

3   Output all the member values and end the program block
```
    print *, achar(10), c_book
end program
```

4   Save the file named as **derive.f90**, then compile and run the program to see the derived type member values

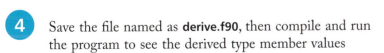

Hot tip

Type structures are used later in this book for Object Oriented Programming (OOP).

```
C:\MyPrograms>derive

C Programming    Mike McGrath                    788457

C:\MyPrograms>
```

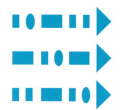

Formatting output

The wildcard * asterisk character in a **print** * statement sends all items in the ensuing comma-separated list to the screen using a default format. The wildcard can, however, be replaced by a format specifier containing "edit descriptors" to format each list item.

Format is specified in a string containing a comma-separated list of edit descriptors within parentheses, with this syntax:

> print '(*descriptor, descriptor, descriptor*)' ..., ..., ...

The edit descriptors can control several features of the format. The symbols below represent the various optional features to control:

- **c** – Column number.
- **d** – Number of digits to the right of a decimal point.
- **m** – Minimum number of digits to display.
- **n** – Number of spaces to skip.
- **r** – Number of times to repeat the descriptor.
- **w** – Width of the output field for the item.

The common edit descriptors are listed in the table below, together with the format of how the features can optionally be controlled:

Hot tip

If the edit descriptor does not explicitly specify the width of the output field, its width will be that of the declaration. For example, **character** without **len** is one space, **integer** without **kind** is 10 spaces.

Beware

Output is, by default, right-aligned in the output field. This means that a string of 10 characters in an output field width of 16 will output six spaces followed by the string.

Item	Item Type	Format	Example
I	Integer	rIw.m	print '(3I2)', a, b, c
F	Real	rFw.d	print '(F6.4)', pi
A	Character	rAw	print '(A10)', str
L	Logical	rLw	print '(L1)', .true.
X	Space	nX	print '(4X, A10)', str
B	Binary	rBw.d	print '(B8.4), a
Z	Hexadecimal	rZw.m	print '(A2, Z12)', '0x', loc(a)
/	Newline	/	print '(/, A10)', str

...cont'd

1 Begin a Fortran program that declares and initializes integer, real, and character constants

```fortran
program main
    implicit none
    integer, parameter :: A = 1, B = 2, C = 3
    real, parameter :: PI = 3.1459
    character(len=10), parameter :: STR = 'Format Fun'
```

format.f90

2 Next, insert statements to output a newline and string, then the string preceded by four spaces

```fortran
    print '(/, A10)', STR
    print '(4X, A10)', STR
```

3 Now, insert a statement to output three integers, each in a output field width of two characters

```fortran
    print '(3I2)', A, B, C
```

4 Add a statement to output a real number in an output field width of six characters, and having four decimal places

```fortran
    print '(F6.4)', PI
```

5 Then, add statements to output a binary number in an output field width of eight characters, and having four places, then a memory address in hexadecimal format

```fortran
    print '(B8.4)', C
    print '(A2,Z12)', '0x', loc(B)
end program
```

6 Save the file named as **format.f90**, then compile and run the program to see the formatted output

```
C:\MyPrograms>format

Format Fun
     Format Fun
 1 2 3
3.1459
     0011
0x7FF7BFA9C4D0

C:\MyPrograms>
```

Where numeric values overflow the specified output field width, the field will be filled with * asterisk characters. Where character strings overflow the specified output field width, the string will be truncated.

23

The length of the memory address in hexadecimal depends on the computer architecture. Here, the length is 12 digits, which corresponds to 48 bits. This is common on 64-bit systems where 48 bits are used for memory addressing, leaving the remaining bits for other purposes.

Summary

- Fortran has been frequently updated to ensure it will continue to meet the demands of modern computing.

- The Intel Fortran Compiler (ifx) fully supports Fortran 2018 and some features of Fortran 2023.

- The free-form file format was introduced in Fortran 90, and is now the preferred format for Fortran program files (**.f90**).

- A Fortran program block begins with the **program** keyword followed by the program name – typically, the name "main".

- The specification section of a program should always include the **implicit none** keywords to ensure declarations are explicit.

- Comments begin with an ! exclamation character.

- A **print** statement sends list-directed output to the screen, and its output can be formatted by edit descriptors.

- A program block ends with the **end program** keywords.

- A variable can be declared as one of the five data types – **integer, real, complex, character, logical**.

- A constant is created by including the **parameter** keyword in its declaration and must be initialized in the declaration.

- The size of **integer** and **real** variables can be dictated by including the **kind** specifier in their declaration.

- A pointer variable is created by including the **pointer** keyword in its declaration and must have memory space allocated.

- The **allocate()** function provides pointer memory space, and the **deallocate()** function frees memory when no longer needed.

- A target variable is created by including the **target** keyword in its declaration, and must be associated with a pointer variable using the **=>** association operator.

- The parts of a complex number can be referenced using its variable name followed by **%re** and **%im** member operations.

- The **abs()** function can be used to return the absolute value of a complex number.

2

Performing operations

This chapter introduces the Fortran operators and demonstrates the operations they can perform.

Doing arithmetic

The arithmetical operators commonly used in Fortran programs are listed in the table below, together with the operation they perform. For the examples below, assume that variable **a** contains the value **8** and variable **b** contains the value **2**.

Operator	Operation	Example
+	Adds two operands	a + b = 10
-	Subtracts the second operand from the first operand	a - b = 6
*	Multiplies both operands	a * b = 16
/	Divides the first operand by the second operand	a / b = 4
**	Raises the first operand to the power of the second operand	a ** b = 64

The operators for addition, subtraction, multiplication, and division act as you would expect, assigning their result using the = assignment operator. Care must be taken, however, to bracket expressions where more than one operator is used to clarify the expression – operations within innermost parentheses are performed first:

```
a = b - c * d / e          ! This is unclear.

a = ( b - c ) * ( d / e )  ! This is clearer.
```

Fortran does not have modulo operator but provides instead an intrinsic **mod()** function that takes two numeric arguments in its parentheses. The **mod()** function will divide the first given number by the second given number and return the remainder of the operation. This is useful to determine if a number has an odd or an even value:

```
integer(kind=1) :: num, remainder

num = 4
remainder = mod(num 2)     ! remainder = 0. Number is even.

num = 5
remainder = mod(num, 2)    ! remainder = 1. Number is odd.
```

1 Begin a Fortran program that declares two small integer variables, plus a character constant to format output

```fortran
program main
    implicit none
    integer(kind=1) :: a, b
    character(len=20), parameter :: LIST = '(A,I2,A2,I2,A,I3)'
```

arith.f90

2 Next, initialize the integer variables with values

```fortran
a = 8
b = 4
```

3 Now, add statements to perform arithmetical operations using the variable values and output the results

```fortran
print *
print LIST, 'Addition ', a, '+', b, ':', a+b
print LIST, 'Subtract', a, '-', b, ':', a-b
print LIST, 'Multiply', a, '*', b, ':', a*b
print LIST, 'Division ', a, '/', b, ':', a/b,
print LIST, 'Modulus ', a, '/', b, ' Remainder:', mod(a,b)
```

Hot tip

Creating a list of edit descriptors as a **character** constant simplifies the output statements. The **print *** statement is then used to output an initial newline character.

4 Assign a new value to one variable and perform one more arithmetical operation, then end the program

```fortran
b = 3
print LIST, 'Modulus ', a, '/', b, ' Remainder:', mod(a,b)
end program
```

5 Save the file named as **arith.f90**, then compile and run the program to see the output from arithmetical operations

```
Intel(r) oneAPI                          — □ X

C:\MyPrograms>ifx /nologo arith.f90

C:\MyPrograms>arith

Addition 8 + 4: 12
Subtract 8 - 4:  4
Multiply 8 * 4: 32
Division 8 / 4:  2
Modulus  8 / 4  Remainder:  0
Modulus  8 / 3  Remainder:  2

C:\MyPrograms>
```

Hot tip

You can, optionally, include a **/nologo** "switch" when compiling programs to inhibit output of the compiler information.

27

Making comparisons

The relational operators that are commonly used in Fortran programming to compare two numerical values are listed in the table below. The programmer can use either form of operator. The legacy form of operator can be found in older Fortran code but the modern form is now preferred as its syntax aligns with other programming languages.

Modern Operator	Legacy Operator	Comparative Test
==	.eq.	Equal
/=	.ne.	Not Equal
>	.gt.	Greater Than
<	.lt.	Less Than
>=	.ge.	Greater than or Equal
<=	.le.	Less than or Equal

Hot tip

A-Z uppercase characters have ASCII code values 65-90 and a-z lowercase characters have ASCII code values 97-122.

The == Equal operator compares two operands and returns .**true.** (printed as **T**) if both are equal in value, otherwise it returns .**false.** (printed as **F**). If both are the same number, they are equal, or if both are characters, their ASCII code values are compared numerically. Conversely, the /= Not Equal operator returns .**true.** if two operands are not equal, using the same rules as the == Equal operator, otherwise it returns .**false.** . Equality operators are useful in testing the state of two variables to perform "conditional branching" in a program.

The > Greater Than operator compares two operands and will return true (**T**) if the first is greater in value than the second, or it will return false (**F**) if it is equal or less in value. The < Less Than operator makes the same comparison but returns true (**T**) if the first operand is less in value than the second, otherwise it returns false (**F**). A > Greater Than or < Less Than operator is often used to test the value of an iteration counter in a loop. Adding the = operator after a > Greater Than or < Less Than operator makes it also return true (**T**) if the two operands are exactly equal in value.

1 Begin a Fortran program that declares several variables, plus a character constant to format output

relate.f90

```fortran
program main
    implicit none
    integer(kind=1) :: nil, num, top
    character(len=1) :: cap, low
    character(len=20), parameter :: LIST = '(A20,A10,L3)'
```

2 Next, initialize the variables with values

```fortran
    nil = 0
    num = 0
    top = 1
    cap = 'A'
    low = 'a'
```

3 Now, add statements to perform relational comparisons of the variable values, then end the program

```fortran
    print *
    print LIST, 'Equal', '0 == 0 :', nil == num
    print LIST, 'Equal', 'A == a :', cap == low
    print LIST, 'Unequal',  '0 /= 1 :', nil /= top
    print LIST, 'Greater',  '0 > 1  :',  nil > top
    print LIST, 'Less Than', '0 < 1  :', nil < top
    print LIST, 'Greater or Equal',   '0 >= 0 :', nil >= num
    print LIST, 'Less Than or Equal', '1 <= 0 :', top <= num
end program
```

4 Save the file named as **relate.f90**, then compile and run the program to see the output results of relational comparison operations

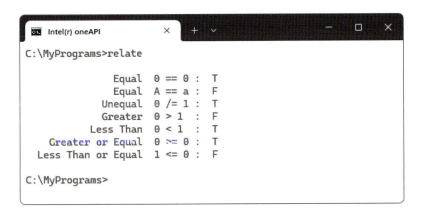

```
Intel(r) oneAPI        ×   +  ⌄              —  □  ×

C:\MyPrograms>relate

             Equal  0 == 0 :   T
             Equal  A == a :   F
           Unequal  0 /= 1 :   T
           Greater  0 > 1  :   F
         Less Than  0 < 1  :   T
  Greater or Equal  0 >= 0 :   T
Less Than or Equal  1 <= 0 :   F

C:\MyPrograms>
```

Don't forget

The ASCII code value for uppercase **'A'** is 65, but for lowercase **'a'** it's 97 – so their comparison here returns false (**F**).

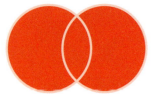

A .and. B

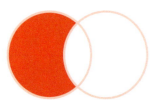

A .or. B

A .and. (.not. B)

The term "Boolean" refers to a system of logical thought developed by the English mathematician George Boole (1815-1864).

Assessing logic

Boolean true and false values in Fortran are represented by logical constants .**true**. and .**false**. The logical operators in Fortran programming are listed in the table below. For the examples, assume that variable **a** contains the value .**true**. and variable **b** contains the value .**false**. .

Operator	Operation	Example
.and.	Logical AND	a.and.b is False
.or.	Logical OR	a.or.b is True
.not.	Logical NOT	.not.a is False
.eqv.	Logical EQUIVALENT	a.eqv.b is False
.neqv.	Logical NON-EQUIVALENT	a.neqv.b is True

The logical operators are used with operands that have Boolean values of true or false, or are values that convert to true or false.

The .**and**. operator evaluates two operands and returns true only if both operands themselves are true. Otherwise, the .**and**. operator returns false. This is used in conditional branching where the direction of a program is determined by testing two conditions – if both conditions are satisfied, the program will go in a certain direction, otherwise it will take a different direction.

Unlike the .**and**. operator that needs both operands to be true, the .**or**. operator evaluates its two operands and returns true if either one of the operands itself returns true. If neither operand returns true then the .**or**. operator returns false. This is useful to perform a certain action if either one of two test conditions has been met.

The .**not**. operator can be used before a single operand to return the inverse value of the given operand. The .**not**. operator is useful to toggle the value of a variable in successive loop iterations to ensure that on each iteration the value is changed, like flicking a light switch on and off.

The .**eqv**. and .**neqv**. operators are useful to compare two expressions for the same logical value.

1 Begin a Fortran program that initializes three constants

```fortran
program main
    implicit none
    logical, parameter :: A = .true., B = .false.
    character(len=30), parameter :: LIST = &
        (/,A12,A12,L2,A12,L2,A12,L2)'
```

logic.f90

2 Add a statement to perform logical AND comparisons

```fortran
print list, 'Logical AND:', 'a AND a :', a.and.a, &
'a AND b :', a.and.b, 'b AND b :', b.and.b
```

3 Add a statement to perform logical OR comparisons

```fortran
print list, 'Logical OR: ', 'a OR a :', a.or.a, &
'a OR b :', a.or.b, 'b OR b :', b.or.b
```

Notice the use of the & line continuation operator in this example.

4 Add a statement to perform logical NOT comparisons

```fortran
print list, 'Logical NOT:', 'a :', a, 'NOT a :', .not.a
```

5 Now, add a statement to perform logical comparison of two expressions, then end the program

```fortran
print '(/,A12,A26,L2)', 'Equivalence:', &
'(5 > 4) .eqv. (8 < 9) :', (5 > 4) .eqv. (8 < 9)
end program
```

6 Save the file named as **logic.f90**, then compile and run the program to see the output results of logical comparisons

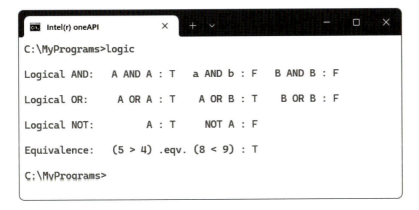

```
Intel(r) oneAPI                     ×    +  ∨      —   □   ×

C:\MyPrograms>logic

Logical AND:    A AND A : T    a AND b : F    B AND B : F

Logical OR:     A OR A : T     A OR B : T     B OR B : F

Logical NOT:       A : T        NOT A : F

Equivalence:    (5 > 4) .eqv. (8 < 9) : T

C:\MyPrograms>
```

Manipulating bits

In computer terms, each byte comprises eight bits that can each contain a **1** or a **0** to store a binary number, representing decimal values from 0 to 255. Each bit contributes a decimal component only when that bit contains a **1**. Components are designated right-to-left from the "Least Significant Bit" (LSB) to the "Most Significant Bit" (MSB). The binary number in the bit pattern below is **00110010** and represents the decimal number 50 (2+16+32):

Bit No.	8 MSB	7	6	5	4	3	2	1 LSB
Decimal	128	64	32	16	8	4	2	1
Binary	0	0	1	1	0	0	1	0

It is possible to manipulate individual bit parts of a byte using the Fortran "bitwise" logical operators listed below:

Operator	Name	Example
.iand.	Bitwise AND	0011 .iand. 0101 = 0001
.ior.	Bitwise OR	0011 .ior. 0101 = 0111
.ieor.	Bitwise Exclusive OR	0011 .ieor. 0101 = 0110
.not.	Bitwise NOT	.not. 0101 = 1010

Hot tip

Each half of a byte is known as a "nibble" (four bits). The binary numbers in the examples in the table describe values stored in a nibble.

The **.iand.** operator compares each bit of two integers and sets a bit to 1 if that bit value in each integer is also 1, otherwise the bit is set to 0.

0011
0101
0001

The **.ior.** operator compares each bit of two integers and sets a bit to 1 if that bit value in either integer is also 1, otherwise the bit is set to 0.

0011
0101
0111

The **.ieor.** operator compares each bit of two integers and sets a bit to 1 if that bit value in each integer is the same, otherwise the bit is set to 0.

0011
0101
0110

The **.not.** operator simply reverses each bit value.

0101
1010

1 Begin a Fortran program that declares two small integer variables, plus two character constants to format output

```fortran
program main
    implicit none
    integer(kind=1) :: a, b
    character(len=12), parameter :: HEAD = '(/,A,I,B8.4)'
    character(len=10), parameter :: LIST = '(A,I,B8.4)'
```

swap.f90

2 Next, initialize the integer variables with values, then display each value in both decimal and binary format

```fortran
    a = 4
    b = 8

    print HEAD, 'a:', a , a
    print LIST, 'b:', b , b
```

3 Add statements to manipulate each variable's bit values

```fortran
    a = ieor(a, b)
    print HEAD, 'a:', a , a
    b = ieor(a, b)
    print LIST, 'b:', b , b
    a = ieor(a, b)
```

In this example, the edit descriptor **B8.4** within the format specifier list specifies that the output should be 8 spaces wide and display the last 4 bits of the binary number.

4 Display each variable value once more in both decimal and binary format, then end the program

```fortran
    print HEAD, 'a:', a , a
    print LIST, 'b:', b , b
end program
```

5 Save the file named as **swap.f90**, then compile and run the program to see the manipulated output results

```
Intel(r) oneAPI

C:\MyPrograms>swap

a:      4      0100
b:      8      1000

a:     12      1100
b:      4      0100

a:      8      1000
b:      4      0100

C:\MyPrograms>
```

Recognizing order

Operator precedence determines the order in which Fortran evaluates expressions. For example, in the expression:
a = 6 + 2 * 3, the order of precedence determines that multiplication is completed first (i.e. **a = 12**, not **a = 24**).

The table below lists operator precedence in descending order – those on the top row have highest precedence; those on lower rows have successively lower precedence.

The order in which Fortran evaluates expressions containing multiple operators of equal precedence is determined by "operator associativity" – grouping operands with the one on the left (LTR) or on the right (RTL).

Don't forget

The * multiplication operator is on a higher row than the + addition operator – so in the expression **a=6+2*3**, multiplication is completed first, before the addition.

34

Category	Operators	Direction
Exponentiation	**	RTL
Multiplication Division	* /	LTR
Addition Subtraction	+ -	LTR
Concatenation	//	LTR
Relational	> >= == < <= /=	LTR
Logical NOT	.not.	LTR
Logical AND	.and.	LTR
Logical OR	.or.	LTR
Logical XOR Logical EQV Logical NEQV	.xor. .eqv. .neqv.	LTR
Logical Bitwise NOT Logical Bitwise AND Logical Bitwise OR Logical Bitwise XOR	.not. .iand. .ior. .ieor.	LTR

1 Begin a Fortran program that declares one small variable, plus a character constant to format output

order.f90

```fortran
program main
    implicit none
    integer(kind=1) :: num
    character(len=10), parameter :: LIST = '(/,A20,I4)'
```

2 Next, add statements that evaluate an expression and output the result

```fortran
    num = 1+4*3
    print LIST, 'Default Order:', num
```

3 Now, add parentheses to edit the expression, then output the modified result

```fortran
    num = (1+4)*3
    print LIST, 'Forced Order:', num
```

4 Then, add statements to evaluate a new expression and output the result

```fortran
    num = 7-4+2
    print LIST, 'Default Direction:', num
```

5 Finally, add parentheses to edit the new expression, then output the modified result and end the program

```fortran
    num=7-(4+2)
    print LIST, 'Forced Direction:', num
end program
```

6 Save the file named as **order.f90**, then compile and run the program to see the default and modified output

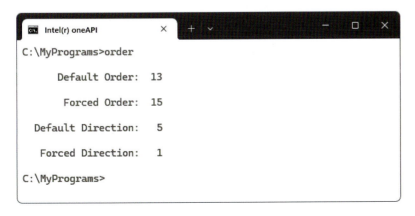

```
Intel(r) oneAPI

C:\MyPrograms>order

        Default Order:   13

        Forced Order:   15

    Default Direction:    5

    Forced Direction:    1

C:\MyPrograms>
```

Casting types

Any data stored in a variable can be forced (coerced) into a variable of a different data type by a process known as "casting".

The cast statement uses the following intrinsic functions that accept the variable to be cast as their argument:

- **int()** – converts an argument of data type **real** or **complex** to an integer. A **real** number argument will produce an **integer** truncated as a whole number. A **complex** number argument will produce an **integer** of the real part truncated.

- **real()** – converts an argument of data type **integer** or **complex** to an integer. An **integer** number argument will produce a **real** number of the default size. A **complex** number argument will produce a **real** number of the real part.

- **char()** – converts an argument of data type **integer** to its corresponding character in the ASCII character set, or processor-defined character set.

Additionally, the second part of a complex number can be output:

- **aimag()** – accepts an argument of data type **complex** and returns its imaginary part as a **real** number.

Casting is often necessary to accurately store the result of an arithmetic operation, because dividing one integer by another integer will always produce an integer result. For example, the integer division **7/2** produces the truncated integer result of **3**.

To store the accurate floating-point result would require integer operands to first be cast into the **real** data type, and the result assigned to a variable of the **real** data type, like this:

```
integer, parameter :: a = 7, b = 2
real(kind=4) :: result

result = real( a ) / real( b )
```

Alternatively, one of the integer operands can simply be multiplied by **1.0** to ensure the division will produce a floating-point result:

```
integer, parameter :: a = 7, b = 2
real(kind=4) :: result

result = ( a * 1.0 ) / b
```

Hot tip

ASCII (pronounced "askee") is the American Standard Code for Information Interchange, which is the accepted standard for plain text. In ASCII, characters are represented numerically within the range 0-127.

1 Begin a Fortran program that declares two variables and three constants

```fortran
program main
    implicit none
    real(kind=4) :: real_num, imag_num
    integer(kind=1), parameter :: INT_NUM = 65
    complex(kind=4), parameter :: PAIR = (16.75, 32.25)
```

cast.f90

2 Next, add statements to initialize a real variable then output the result of casting it as an integer data type

```fortran
    real_num = 16.50
    print '(/,A12,I5)', 'Integer:', int(real_num)
```

3 Now, add statements to output the result of casting an integer value as a real and a character data type

```fortran
    print '(A12,F8.2)', 'Real:', real(INT_NUM)
    print '(A12,A4)', 'Character:', char(INT_NUM)
```

4 Then, add statements to output the real part of the complex number

```fortran
    real_num = real(PAIR)
    print '(A12,F8.2)', 'Complex(1):', real_num
```

5 Finally, add statements to output the imaginary part of the complex number, then end the program

```fortran
    imag_num = aimag(PAIR)
    print '(A12,F8.2)', 'Complex(2):', imag_num
end program
```

6 Save the file named as **cast.f90**, then compile and run the program to see the cast values output

37

Don't forget

The result of dividing an integer by another integer is truncated, not rounded – so a result of 9.9 would become 9.

```
Intel(r) oneAPI

C:\MyPrograms>cast

    Integer:    16
       Real:    65.00
  Character:    A
 Complex(1):    16.75
 Complex(2):    32.25

C:\MyPrograms>
```

Summary

- Fortran supports the usual arithmetical operators plus an ** exponentiation operator that raises a number to a power.

- Fortran does not have a modulus operator but does provide a **mod()** function to determine the remainder after a division.

- Within an expression, operations within innermost ( ) parentheses are performed first.

- Creating a format specifier list of edit descriptors as a **character** constant simplifies **print** output statements.

- The relational operators compare two numerical values for equality or inequality, and for greater or lower value.

- Boolean true and false values in Fortran are represented by logical constants **.true.** and **.false.** .

- Relational operators return **.true.** (printed **T**) or **.false.** (printed **F**) as the result of comparing two numerical values.

- A-Z uppercase characters have ASCII code values 65-90, and a-z lowercase characters have ASCII code values 97-122.

- Logical operators are used with operands that have Boolean values of true or false, or values that convert to true or false.

- A byte comprises eight bits that can each contain a **1** or a **0** to store a binary number, representing decimal 0 to 255.

- Each bit in a binary number contributes a decimal component only when that bit contains a **1**.

- It is possible to manipulate individual bit parts of a byte using the Fortran bitwise logical operators.

- Operator precedence determines the order in which Fortran evaluates expressions.

- Data stored in a variable can be forced (coerced) into a variable of a different data type by casting.

- The parts of a complex number can be returned by the **real()** and **aimag()** functions respectively.

3 Controlling flow

This chapter demonstrates Fortran conditional statements, which allow programs to branch in different directions.

Testing conditions

The Fortran **if** keyword performs the basic conditional test that evaluates a given expression for a Boolean value of true or false. The conditional test must be enclosed within **( )** parentheses and be followed by the Fortran **then** keyword. Statements to be executed when the expression is found to be true form the body of a code block that must be terminated with **end if** keywords. The syntax of the **if** statement block looks like this:

```
if ( test-expression ) then
    statement/s-to-execute-when-true
end if
```

Optionally, an **if** code block can offer alternative statements to execute when the test fails by appending an **else** statement block after the **if** statement block, like this:

```
if ( test-expression ) then
    statement/s-to-execute-when-true
else
    statement/s-to-execute-when-false
end if
```

This operation performs "conditional branching", which allows the program to proceed in different directions according to the result of the conditional test. It can be represented visually by a flowchart:

Hot tip

Shorthand can be used when testing a Boolean value – so the expression **if (flag == .true.)** can be written as **if (flag)**.

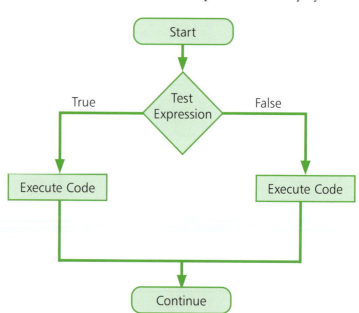

1 Begin a Fortran program that declares a single variable

```fortran
program main
    implicit none
    real(kind=4) :: angle
```

ifelse.f90

2 Next, add a statement to initialize the variable

```fortran
angle = 90.0
```

3 Now, add an **if** code block to test the variable value

```fortran
if (angle == 90.0) then
    print '(/,A,I3,A)', ' Angle: ', int(angle), ' degrees'
    print *, 'Corner is a right angle'
end if
```

4 Then, add a statement to change the variable value

```fortran
angle = angle + 15
```

5 Finally, add an **if-else** code block to test the variable value

```fortran
if (angle < 90.0) then
    print '(/,A,I3,A)', ' Angle: ', int(angle), ' degrees'
    print *, 'Corner is acute'
else
    print '(/,A,I3,A)', ' Angle: ', int(angle), ' degrees'
    print *, 'Corner is obtuse'
end if
```

The body of the **if** and **else** code blocks should be indented for clarity.

6 Save the file named as **ifelse.f90**, then compile and run the program to see the result of conditional branching

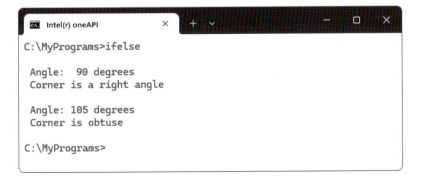

```
Intel(r) oneAPI                    ×    + ∨        —   □   ×

C:\MyPrograms>ifelse

 Angle:  90 degrees
 Corner is a right angle

 Angle: 105 degrees
 Corner is obtuse

C:\MyPrograms>
```

41

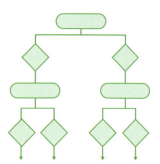

Nesting choices

The Fortran **if** statement can be used to test multiple conditions for a Boolean true or false value in a variety of ways:

- The **.and.** and **.or.** logical operators can be included in a conditional test to evaluate multiple expressions:

```
if ( test-expression .and. test-expression ) then
    statement/s-to-execute-when-true
end if
```

```
if ( test-expression .or. test-expression ) then
    statement/s-to-execute-when-true
end if
```

- The **else** keyword can be followed by a further **if** statement:

```
if ( test-expression ) then
    statement/s-to-execute-when-true
else if ( test-expression ) then
    statement/s-to-execute-when-true
end if
```

- The **if** statement can be followed by a further **if** statement, creating a "nested" structure:

```
if ( test-expression ) then
    if ( test-expression ) then
        statement/s-to-execute-when-true
    end if
end if
```

nest.f90

1. Begin a Fortran program that declares three integer constants
```
program main
    implicit none
    integer(kind=1), parameter :: X = 8, Y = 16, Z = 32
```

2. Add a statement to evaluate two expressions that will succeed if either expression is true
```
print *
if (X < 5 .or. Y < 20) then
    print *, '1. Test successful!'
else
    print *, '1. Test failure!'
end if
```

...cont'd

3 Next, add a statement to evaluate three expressions that will only succeed if all expressions are true

```
if (X < 10 .and. Y < 20 .and. Z > 20) then
    print *, '2. All tests succeeded'
else
    print *, '2. Not all tests succeeded'
end if
```

4 Now, add statements to evaluate three expressions that will succeed if any of the expressions are true

```
if (X > 10) then
    print *, '3. first test succeeded'
else if (Y > 15) then
    print *, '3. second test succeeded'
else if (Z > 20) then
    print *, '3. third test succeeded'
else
    print *, '3. No test succeeded'
end if
```

Notice that evaluation ends when a test succeeds. Here, the third test would succeed but is never evaluated.

5 Then, add nested statements to evaluate three expressions that will only succeed if all expressions are true

```
if (X < 10) then
    if (Y < 20) then
        if (Z > 40) then
            print *, '4. All tests succeeded'
        else
            print *, '4. Not all tests succeeded'
        end if
    end if
end if
end program
```

Three levels of nested **if** statements are generally considered the maximum for good code design.

6 Save the file named as **nest.f90**, then compile and run the program to see the result of multiple conditional tests

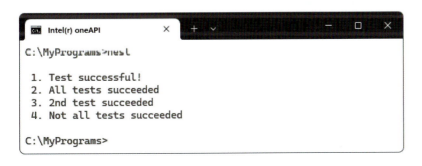

Selecting case

The **if** and **else** keywords, introduced on pages 42-43, allow programs to branch in a particular direction according to the result of a test condition, and can be used to repeatedly test a variable to match a value. For example, testing for an integer:

```
if ( num == 1 )
    print *, 'Monday'
else if ( num == 2 )
    print *, 'Tuesday'
else if ( num == 3 )
    print * 'Wednesday'
else if ( num == 4 )
    print *, 'Thursday'
else if ( num == 5 )
    print * 'Friday'
end if
```

The program will branch in the direction of the match.

Conditional branching with long **if else** statements can often be more efficiently performed using a **select case** statement instead, especially when the test expression evaluates one variable.

The **select case** statement works in an unusual way. It takes a given variable value, then seeks a matching value among a number of **case** statements. Statements associated with the matching **case** statement value will then be executed.

When no match is found, no **case** statements will be executed, but you may add a **case default** statement to specify statements to be executed when no match is found.

The body of a **select case** code block must be terminated with **end select** keywords. The syntax of a **select case** block looks like this:

```
select case ( variable-name )
    case ( value-1 )
        statement/s-to-be-executed
    case ( value-2 )
        statement/s-to-be-executed
    case ( value-3 )
        statement/s-to-be-executed
    case default
        statement/s-to-be-executed
end select
```

Evaluation of **case** statements in the **select case** block ends immediately when a match is found.

Hot tip

A **case** statement can use extent specifiers to match any value from a range of values. For example, **case(1:5)** will match any value between 1 and 5 inclusive.

Hot tip

Note that a **case default** statement always appears last in a **select case** statement.

1 Begin a Fortran program that declares two variables

```fortran
program main
    implicit none
    integer(kind=1) :: marks
    real(kind=4) :: rand_num
```

select.f90

2 Next, add statements to initialize the integer variable with a random value between 0 and 100

```fortran
call random_seed()
call random_number(rand_num)
marks = int(rand_num * 100) + 1
print *, 'Your marks:', marks
```

Hot tip

3 Now, add a **select case** block to examine the integer variable, and output a statement when a match is found

```fortran
select case(marks)
    case(81:100)
        print *, 'Excellent!'
    case(61:80)
        print *, 'Well Done!'
    case(41:60)
        print *, 'Poor Attempt!'
    case(1:40)
        print *, 'Failure!'
    case default
        print *, 'Invalid Marks'
end select
end program
```

The **call** to the Fortran's intrinsic **random_seed()** function initializes its random number generator to ensure it will generate different sequences. The **call** to the **random_number()** function generates a pseudo-random number between 0 (inclusive) and 1 (exclusive). Multiplying this by 100 creates a number from 0-99 and adding 1 changes the range to 1-100.

45

4 Save the file named as **select.f90**, then compile and run the program to see output for matching cases

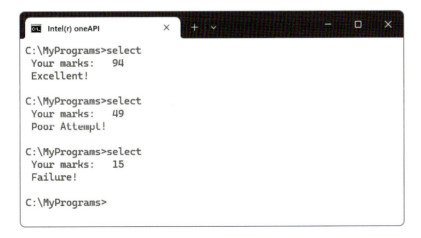

```
Intel(r) oneAPI
C:\MyPrograms>select
 Your marks:    94
 Excellent!

C:\MyPrograms>select
 Your marks:    49
 Poor Attempt!

C:\MyPrograms>select
 Your marks:    15
 Failure!

C:\MyPrograms>
```

Do looping

A loop is a piece of code in a program that automatically repeats. One complete execution of all statements contained within the loop block is known as an "iteration" or "pass".

The number of iterations made by a loop is specified by the statement at start the loop. The two types of loop structures in Fortran programming are **do** loops and **do while** loops.

A **do** loop begins by initializing an integer variable with an initial "counter" value, then specifies a final counter value. The loop body contains one or more statements to be executed on each iteration of the loop. The body of a **do** loop code block must be terminated with **end do** keywords, so its syntax looks like this:

```
do variable-name start , stop
    statement/s to be executed
end do
```

The counter variable is traditionally named "i". The **do** loop increments the counter by 1 on each iteration by default, and the loop ends when the counter exceeds the specified final value. Optionally, the **do** statement can specify an alternative value by which the loop counter should be incremented on each iteration:

```
do variable-name start , stop , step
    statement/s to be executed
end do
```

Loops may be nested within other loops – so that the inner loop will fully execute its iterations on each iteration of the outer loop:

```
do variable-name-1 start , stop
    statement/s to be executed by the outer loop

    do variable-name-2 start , stop
        statement/s to be executed by the inner loop
    end do

end do
```

With nested loops, the entire loop ends when the variable counter of the outer loop exceeds its specified final value.

Hot tip

A **do while** loop is described and demonstrated in the example on page 48.

46

1 Begin a Fortran program that declares two variables

```
program main
    implicit none
    integer(kind=1) :: i, j
```

doloop.f90

2 Next, add a loop that will make five iterations and output its counter value on each iteration

```
print *
do i = 1, 5
    print *, 'Iteration: ', i
end do
```

3 Now, add nested loops that will each output their respective counter value on each iteration

```
do i = 1, 2
    print '(/,A,I3)', 'Outer Loop:', i
    do j = 2, 6, 2
        print *, 'Inner Loop: ', j
    end do
end do
end program
```

4 Save the file named as **doloop.f90**, then compile and run the program to see the loop counter values

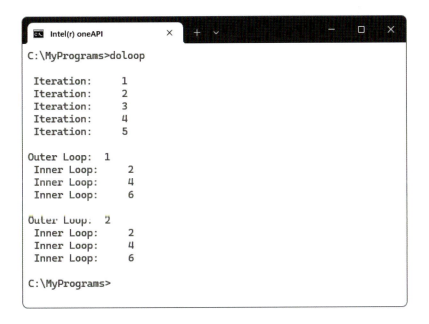

```
C:\MyPrograms>doloop

Iteration:      1
Iteration:      2
Iteration:      3
Iteration:      4
Iteration:      5

Outer Loop:  1
  Inner Loop:      2
  Inner Loop:      4
  Inner Loop:      6

Outer Loop:  2
  Inner Loop:      2
  Inner Loop:      4
  Inner Loop:      6

C:\MyPrograms>
```

After the fifth iteration of the first loop, the counter value has reached its final value, so the loop ends.

47

Looping while

In addition to the simple **do** loop in the previous example, which explicitly specifies the number of iterations to perform, Fortran provides a **do while** loop structure.

A **do while** loop begins by evaluating a test condition for a true or false value. When the evaluation is found to be true, the loop will perform an iteration to execute any statements in the loop body. If the evaluation is found to be false, the loop will end. Like the simple **do** loop, a **do while** loop code block must also be terminated by an **end do** statement.

In order for a **do while** loop to run at all, the test condition must first be true. Most importantly, the **do while** loop body <u>must</u> contain a statement that will, at some point, affect the tested expression in order to change the evaluation result to become false – otherwise, an infinite loop is created that will lock the system! For example, where a **do while** loop tests the value of a counter integer at the start of each iteration, the loop body <u>must</u> contain a statement to increment or decrement the counter on each iteration.

The syntax of a **do while** loop that tests the value of an incrementing counter on each iteration looks like this:

```
do while ( variable-name < maximum-value )
    statement/s to be executed
    increment-variable-name
end do
```

The tested condition need not test a counter value; the expression could be any expression that can evaluate to true or false.

The decision to use a simple **do** loop or a **do while** loop is often a matter of personal preference, but the distinction between them is that a **do** loop is controlled by a counter within a known range, whereas a **do while** loop is controlled by a condition evaluated before each iteration.

Often, however, either loop structure can be used. For example, to output factorial values – the product of all positive integers less than or equal to **n**. When **n**=4, factorial is: **4 * 3 * 2 * 1 = 24**.

Hot tip

If you accidentally start running an infinite loop, press the **Ctrl** + **C** keys to terminate the process.

1 Begin a Fortran program that declares three variables

```fortran
program main
   implicit none
   integer(kind=1) :: num
   integer(kind=4) :: factorial, previous_num
```

while.f90

2 Next, add statements to initialize each variable

```fortran
num = 1
factorial = 1
previous_num = 1
```

3 Add a loop to output an incrementing list of factorials from 1 to 10

```fortran
print *
do while (num < 11)
   factorial = factorial * num
   num = num + 1
   print *, num-1, 'x', previous_num, '=', factorial
   previous_num = factorial
end do
end program
```

4 Save the file named as **while.f90**, then compile and run the program to see the loop output factorial values

```
Intel(r) oneAPI                    ×    +  ⌄        —  □  ×

C:\MyPrograms>while

          1 x          1 =          1
          2 x          1 =          2
          3 x          2 =          6
          4 x          6 =         24
          5 x         24 =        120
          6 x        120 =        720
          7 x        720 =       5040
          8 x       5040 =      40320
          9 x      40320 =     362880
         10 x     362880 =    3628800

C:\MyPrograms>
```

Breaking out

The Fortran **cycle** keyword can be used to skip a single iteration of a loop when a specified condition is met. The **cycle** statement is situated inside the loop statement block and is preceded by a test expression. When the test returns true, that single iteration ends.

cycle.f90

1 Begin a Fortran program that declares two variables
```fortran
program main
    implicit none
    integer(kind=1) :: i, j
```

2 Next, add nested loops that will each output their respective counter value on each iteration
```fortran
    do i = 1, 2
        print '(/,A,I3)', 'Outer Loop:', i
        do j = 2, 6, 2
            ! Conditional test to be inserted here.
            print *, 'Inner Loop: ', j
        end do
    end do
end program
```

3 Now, insert a conditional test to skip an iteration
```fortran
        if (i == 1 .and. j == 4) then
            print *, 'Loop cycles at i=1 and j=4'
            cycle
        end if
```

4 Save the file named as **cycle.f90**, then compile and run the program to see the loop counter values

```
Intel(r) oneAPI                    ×    + ∨         —    □    ×

C:\MyPrograms>cycle

Outer Loop:   1
 Inner Loop:      2
 Loop cycles at i=1 and j=4
 Inner Loop:      6

Outer Loop:   2
 Inner Loop:      2
 Inner Loop:      4
 Inner Loop:      6

C:\MyPrograms>
```

...cont'd

The **exit** keyword can be used to prematurely terminate a loop when a specified condition is met. The **exit** statement is situated inside the loop statement block, and is preceded by a test expression. When the test returns true the loop ends immediately.

1   Begin a Fortran program that declares two variables

breaks.f90

```fortran
program main
    implicit none
    integer(kind=1) :: i, j
```

2   Next, add nested loops that will each output their respective counter value on each iteration

```fortran
do i = 1, 2
    print '(/,A,I3)', 'Outer Loop:', i
    do j = 2, 6, 2
        ! Conditional test to be inserted here.
        print *, 'Inner Loop: ', j
    end do
end do
end program
```

3   Now, insert a conditional test to skip an iteration

```fortran
if (i == 2 .and. j == 4) then
    print *, 'Loop exits at i=2 and j=4'
    exit
end if
```

4   Save the file named as **breaks.f90**, then compile and run the program to see the loop counter values

```
Intel(r) oneAPI          ×     +  ∨              —   □   ×

C:\MyPrograms>breaks

Outer Loop:  1
 Inner Loop:        2
 Inner Loop:        4
 Inner Loop:        6

Outer Loop:  2
 Inner Loop:        2
 Loop exits at i=2 and j=4

C:\MyPrograms>
```

Summary

- The **if** keyword performs a basic conditional test to evaluate a given expression for a Boolean value of true or false.

- The **else** keyword can be used to provide alternative statements to execute when an **if** statement evaluates an expression as false.

- Offering a program alternative directions in which to proceed following an evaluation is known as conditional branching.

- Loops can evaluate multiple conditional tests using **else if** keywords or by nesting multiple **if** code blocks.

- All **if** code blocks must be terminated by the **end if** keywords.

- Conditional branching performed by multiple **if else** statements can often be performed efficiently by a **select case** statement.

- Optionally, a **select case** block may include a final **case default** statement with statements to execute when no match is found.

- A **do** loop specifies the number of iterations to perform by initializing a counter variable and by specifying a final value.

- A **do** loop increments its counter variable on each iteration.

- A **do** loop ends when the counter exceeds the final value.

- A **do while** loop evaluates a test condition for a true or false value and will perform iterations when the test is true.

- The body of a **do while** loop must contain a statement that will at some point cause its conditional test to become false.

- A **do while** loop ends when the test condition is false.

- All **do** loop and **do while** loop blocks must be terminated by the **end do** keywords.

- A loop may contain a conditional test that will skip a single loop iteration using the **cycle** keyword if the test fails.

- A loop may contain a conditional test that will immediately end the loop using the **exit** keyword if the test fails.

4 Handling strings

This chapter demonstrates

how to manipulate Fortran

character text strings.

Resizing strings

The **character** data type has, by default, a length of 1. Strings are just multiple consecutive characters of a length specified by the **len** specifier in the **character** variable declaration. Each individual character in a string can be referenced by its position in the string. The first (leftmost) character in a string is at position 1, the second character is at position 2, and so on.

Declaring **character** string variables of a specified length allows the program to assign string values of that length as the program proceeds. Assigning shorter string values will retain the character space width though, and assigning longer string values will simply truncate the long string at the variable's specified length.

Usefully, a **character** string variable can be allowed to resize as the program proceeds by declaring it with the **allocatable** keyword. The declaration can include a **len** specifier assigned a : colon character to indicate that its length can be varied. The syntax of a resizable **character** string variable looks like this:

```
character( len=: ), allocatable :: variable-name
```

Hot tip

Optionally, the **len=** part of the length specifier can be omitted, so can become **character(:)**.

When the program no longer needs an **allocatable** variable, its memory space must be freed by specifying the variable name to the intrinsic **deallocate()** function. Multiple variable names can be specified as arguments to this function in a comma-separated list:

```
deallocate( variable-name1, variable-name2 )
```

The current length of a variable can be found by specifying the variable name as the argument to the intrinsic **len()** function.

Multiple strings can be combined into a single string using the Fortran **//** concatenation operator. For example:

Hot tip

Memory space can also be specified without assigning a string value by an **allocate()** function. For example: **allocate(character(len=**n**) :: variable-name)**.

```
string1 = 'news'
string2 = 'cast'
string3 = string1//string2        ! newscast
```

The **//** concatenation operator can be used to output multiple strings as a combined string. It is, however, important to recognize that the strings are only combined into a single string in an assignment.

1 Begin a Fortran program that declares two resizable character string variables

```
program main
    implicit none
    character(len=:), allocatable :: str1, str2
```

string.f90

2 Next, initialize both character variables

```
    str1 = 'John'
    str2 = 'Boy'
```

3 Now, output the strings and their length

```
    print '(/,A,X1A)', str1, str2
    print '(A8,I2,A16,I2)', 'Length1:', len(str1), &
        'Length2:', len(str2)
```

4 Then, assign new strings to the character variables

```
    str1 = 'bitter'
    str2 = 'sweet'
```

5 Output the new strings in concatenated form, then output each character variable's resized length

```
    print '(/,A)', str1//str2
    print '(A8,I2,A16,I2)', 'Length1:', len(str1), &
        'Length2:', len(str2)
```

6 Finally, free the memory space and end the program

```
    deallocate(str1, str2)
end program
```

7 Save the file named as **string.f90**, then compile and run the program to see the resizing character variables

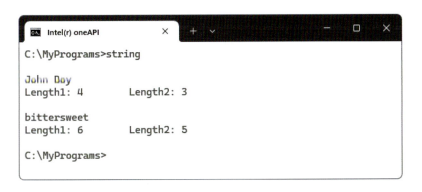

```
C:\MyPrograms>string

John Boy
Length1: 4         Length2: 3

bittersweet
Length1: 6         Length2: 5

C:\MyPrograms>
```

Extracting substrings

A "substring" can be extracted from a **character** string by specifying its start and end index position within the string. These are stated as a colon-separated argument within parentheses after the character string variable's name. The syntax looks like this:

> variable-name(*start-position* : *end-position*)

An individual character can be referenced by stating its position at each side of the colon in the argument:

> variable-name(*position* : *position*)

In each case, this form of index specification is called an "extent specifier" in Fortran, and is known as a "slice" in other languages.

Optionally, values can be omitted from the extent specifier where all characters to the boundary of the string are required. For example, all characters up to, and including, position 5:

> variable-name(: 5)

Alternatively, all characters starting at, and including, position 5:

> variable-name(5 :)

An extent specifier can also be assigned new characters to replace a substring within a string:

> variable-name(2 : 6) = new-characters

A **character** string can be searched to see if it contains a specified "substring" using an **index()** function. This function requires the string variable name as its first argument, and the substring to seek number as its second argument:

> index(*variable-name, substring-to-seek*)

When a search successfully locates the specified substring, the **index()** function returns the index number of the first occurrence of the substring's first character within the searched string. When the search fails, the **index()** function returns a value of **0** to indicate failure.

...cont'd

1 Begin a Fortran program that declares a character variable
```fortran
program main
    implicit none
    character(len=20) :: string
```

extract.f90

2 Initialize the string, then output its value and a substring
```fortran
string = 'The sun and moon.'
print '(/,A)', string
print *,'Extracted substring:', string(13:16)
```

3 Next, search for two substrings within the string
```fortran
if (index(string, 'sun') /= 0 ) then
    print '(1X,A,I3)', ' "sun" found at:', index(string, 'sun')
end if

if (index(string, 'stars') == 0 ) then
    print *, ' "stars" not found'
end if
```

4 Now, assign a new substring to the end part of the string and output the modified string
```fortran
string(5:) = 'moon and stars.'
print '(/,A)', string
```

Don't forget

5 Search for a substring within the modified string, then end the program
```fortran
print '(A,I3)', ' "stars" found at:', index(string, 'stars')
end program
```

6 Save the file named as **extract.f90,** then compile and run the program to see the substring extractions and searches

To include quote marks within a string they must differ from the ones used to enclose the string – double quotes within single quotes, or single quotes within double quotes.

```
Intel(r) oneAPI                    ×    +  ∨           –  □  ×

C:\MyPrograms>extract

The sun and moon.
 Extracted substring:moon
  "sun" found at:   5
  "stars" not found

The moon and stars.
 "stars" found at: 14

C:\MyPrograms>
```

Examining strings

The **len()** function can be used to return the length of a character string specified as its argument as an integer. By default, the result will be an integer of four bytes in size but optionally, the **len()** function can accept a **kind** argument to specify the return size:

result = len(*string-variable-name*, kind= *n*)

To determine the length of a character string excluding any trailing blank spaces, the **len_trim()** function can be used. This, too, returns an integer whose size can, optionally, be specified by including a **kind** argument:

result = len_trim(*string-variable-name*, kind= *n*)

The Fortran **scan()** function can be used to search a string for the presence of any characters from a specified set of characters. The search begins, by default, at the first (leftmost) character of the string, then examines each character in turn to seek a match with any character in the specified set. When a match is found, the search ends, and the **scan()** function returns an integer that is the position of the matched character within the string. If no match is found, the **scan()** function returns **0**.

result = scan(*string-variable-name*, *character-set*)

Optionally, the **scan()** function can be made to begin its search at the final (rightmost) character of the string by including a **back** argument with an assigned **.true.** value. In this case, the search is made in reverse order, and ends when a match is found. The **scan()** function returns an integer that is the position of the matched character, or if no match is found, the **scan()** function returns **0**.

result = scan(*string-variable-name*, *character-set*, back = .true.)

The **scan()** function may also, optionally, include a **kind** argument to specify the size of the returned integer.

The **verify()** function works in a similar way to the **scan()** function, and accepts all the same arguments. It checks that all characters in the string appear in the specified character set. When a character in the string is absent in the character set, the **verify()** function returns an integer that is the position of the unmatched character. If all characters match, the **verify()** function returns **0**.

The searches made by the **scan()** and **verify()** functions are case sensitive.

1 Begin a Fortran program that declares several variables
```fortran
program main
    implicit none
    character(len=64) :: str
    integer(kind=1) :: n
    character(len=12), parameter :: LIST = '(A,A4,A3,I3)'
```

examine.f90

2 Initialize the string, then output its value and a substring
```fortran
    str = 'I have nothing to declare but my genius.'
    print '(/,A)', str
```

3 Next, output the string variable's size and character length
```fortran
    print *, 'String Allocated Length:', len(str)
    print *, 'String Character Length:', len_trim(str), achar(10)
```

4 Now, search the string to match any character in a set, both forward and backward
```fortran
    n = scan(str, 'abc')
    print LIST, 'Scan for abc:', str(n:n), 'at', n
    n = scan(str, 'abc', back=.true.)
    print LIST, 'Scan back abc:', str(n:n), 'at', n
```

Hot tip

These searches seek to match characters including blank spaces.

5 Check that all characters in a set appear in the string, then end the program
```fortran
    n = verify(str, 'aei hv')
    print LIST, 'Verify "aei hv":', str(n:n), 'at', n
end program
```

6 Save the file named as **examine.f90**, then compile and run the program to see the character set searches

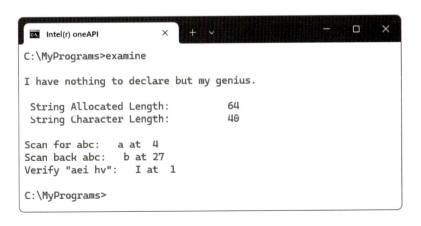

```
Intel(r) oneAPI

C:\MyPrograms>examine

I have nothing to declare but my genius.

 String Allocated Length:        64
 String Character Length:        40

Scan for abc:    a at  4
Scan back abc:    b at 27
Verify "aei hv":   I at  1

C:\MyPrograms>
```

Adjusting strings

The string of characters in a **character** variable are, by default, left-aligned. When the string is less than the size of the **character** variable, the spaces to the right of the string are filled with blank space characters ("trailing" blank spaces). For example, with a **character** variable length of **8** containing a string of **4** characters:

Trailing space can be unwanted in output but can be removed by passing the character string as an argument to the Fortran **trim()** function. This will remove all trailing blank spaces in the output but it is important to recognize that the **trim()** function does not reduce the size of the character variable. For example:

```
print *, trim( str )          ! Outputs TEXT.
print *, len( str )           ! Outputs 8.
```

A trimmed string can, however, be assigned to a character variable of the same length as the trimmed string:

```
print *, len( str2 )          ! Outputs 4.
str2 = trim( str )
print *, str2                 ! Outputs TEXT
```

As integer values are, by default, right-aligned, it is sometimes useful to also output character strings right-aligned – so both are aligned on the screen. This can be achieved by passing the character string as an argument to the Fortran **adjustr()** function. This right-adjusts the character string within the allocated **character** variable size by removing all trailing spaces and inserting the same number of spaces at the beginning of the string.

The Fortran **adjustr()** function has a companion **adjustl()** function that left-adjusts the character string within the allocated **character** variable size by removing all leading spaces from the beginning of the string and inserting the same number of spaces at the end of the string. As with the **trim()** function, the **adjustr()** and **adjustl()** functions do not change the size of the character variable.

1 Begin a Fortran program that declares a character variable and a character constant

adjust.f90

```fortran
program main
    implicit none
    character(len=50) :: str
    character(len=10), parameter :: ORIGIN = '- Hubbard'
```

2 Initialize the string, then output its value, size, and length

```fortran
str = 'When life gives you lemons, make lemonade.'
print '(/,A)', str
print *, 'String Allocated Length:', len(str)
print *, 'String Character Length:', len_trim(str)
print *, '----------'
```

3 Now, adjust the position of the character string within the allocated variable size and output its appearance

```fortran
str = adjustr(str)
print *, str
str = adjustl(str)
print *, str
print *, '----------'
```

4 Output both strings without adjustment, then output the strings without trailing blank spaces and end the program

```fortran
print *, str, ORIGIN
print *, trim(str), ORIGIN
end program
```

5 Save the file named as **adjust.f90**, then compile and run the program to see the adjusted character strings

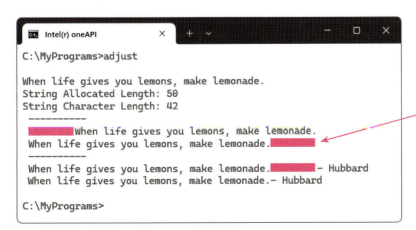

The colored areas here indicate blank spaces.

Converting strings

The intrinsic Fortran **achar()** function can be used to output a newline character by specifying the ASCII character code 10 as its argument. It can also be used to reference other characters in the ASCII table below. Notice that the character code difference between lowercase and uppercase letters is 32. This can be used to convert the case of characters in a string.

The **achar()** function has a companion **iachar()** function that accepts a character as its argument and returns the corresponding ASCII character code.

The intrinsic **repeat()** function is useful to output multiple concatenated copies of a character or string. It requires two arguments to specify the character/s to copy, and the number of copies to produce.

ASCII Table													
0	[NULL]	22	[SYNCHRONOUS IDLE]	44	,	66	B	88	X	110	n
1	[START OF HEADING]	23	[END TRANSMIT BLOCK]	45	-	67	C	89	Y	111	o
2	[START OF TEXT]	24	[CANCEL]	46	.	68	D	90	Z	112	p
3	[END OF TEXT]	25	[END OF MEDIUM]	47	/	69	E	91	[	113	q
4	[END OF TRANSMISSION]	26	[SUBSTITUTE]	48	0	70	F	92	\	114	r
5	[ENQUIRY]	27	[ESCAPE]	49	1	71	G	93	]	115	s
6	[ACKNOWLEDGE]	28	[FILE SEPARATOR]	50	2	72	H	94	^	116	t
7	[BELL]	29	[GROUP SEPARATOR]	51	3	73	I	95	_	117	u
8	[BACKSPACE]	30	[RECORD SEPARATOR]	52	4	74	J	96	`	118	v
9	[HORIZONTAL TAB]	31	[UNIT SEPARATOR]	53	5	75	K	97	a	119	w
10	[LINEFEED]	32	[SPACE]	54	6	76	L	98	b	120	x
11	[VERTICAL TAB]	33	!	55	7	77	M	99	c	121	y
12	[FORM FEED]	34	"	56	8	78	N	100	d	122	z
13	[CARRIAGE RETURN]	35	#	57	9	79	O	101	e	123	{
14	[SHIFT OUT]	36	$	58	:	80	P	102	f	124		
15	[SHIFT IN]	37	%	59	;	81	Q	103	g	125	}
16	[DATA LINK ESCAPE]	38	&	60	<	82	R	104	h	126	~
17	[DEVICE CONTROL 1]	39	'	61	=	83	S	105	i	127	[DEL]
18	[DEVICE CONTROL 2]	40	(	62	>	84	T	106	j		
19	[DEVICE CONTROL 3]	41	)	63	?	85	U	107	k		
20	[DEVICE CONTROL 4]	42	*	64	@	86	V	108	l		
21	[NEGATIVE ACKNOWLEDGE]	43	+	65	A	87	W	109	m		

1 Begin a Fortran program that declares three variables

```fortran
program main
    implicit none
    character(len=64) :: str
    integer(kind=1) :: i, char_code
```

convert.f90

2 Initialize the string variable, then output its value

```fortran
str = 'Workers of the world, unite!'
print '(/,1X,A)', str
```

3 Next, add a loop that converts each lowercase character in the string to uppercase, and output the modified string

```fortran
do i = 1, len_trim(str)
    char_code = ichar(str(i:i))
    if (char_code > 96 .and. char_code < 123) then
        str(i:i) = achar(char_code - 32)
    end if
end do
print *, str
```

Conversely, convert from uppercase to lowercase for character codes 65-90 by adding 32.

4 Then, output a string that is a repeated character, and is the same length as the modified string

```fortran
print *, repeat(achar(42), len_trim(str))
```

5 Finally, output a string that confirms the ASCII character code of the repeated character

```fortran
print '(1X,A,I3)', 'The Answer To Everything:', iachar('*')
```

6 Save the file named as **convert.f90**, then compile and run the program to see the converted character strings

```
Intel(r) oneAPI

C:\MyPrograms>convert

Workers of the world, unite!

WORKERS OF THE WORLD, UNITE!

****************************
The Answer To Everything: 42

C:\MyPrograms>
```

63

Dating strings

Fortran provides an intrinsic **data_and_time()** function that returns the current date, time, and timezone from the system clock in these specific formats:

- **Date** – a character string in **YYYYMMDD** format.

- **Time** – a character string in **HHMMSS.SSS** format.

- **Timezone** – a character string in **(+/-)HHMM** format.

The **call** keyword is used to invoke the function with this syntax:

call date_and_time(*date-variable, time-variable, zone-variable*)

Date, time, and timezone information is assigned to the relevant argument variables, then each of their components can be assigned to individual variables using the (:) extent specifier.

datetime.f90

1 Begin a Fortran program that declares variables to store date, time, and timezone information
```
program main
    implicit none
    character(len=8) :: d_str
    character(len=10):: t_str
    character(len=5) :: tz
```

2 Next, declare variables to store individual date and time components
```
    character(len=4) :: y, ms
    character(len=2) :: d, m, hh, mm, ss
```

3 Now, invoke the function to get the information, then output the current timezone
```
    call date_and_time(d_str, t_str, tz )
    print '(/,A,3X,A,A)', 'Timezone: ', 'UTC', tz
```

UTC (Coordinated Universal Time) is also known as GMT (Greenwich Mean Time).

4 Then, output the current date information and assign its individual components to separate variables
```
    print '(A,A)', 'Date String: ', d_str
    y = d_str(1:4)
    m = d_str(5:6)
    d = d_str(7:8)
```

5 Likewise, output the current time information and assign its individual components to separate variables
```
print '(A,A,/)', 'Time String: ', t_str
hh = t_str(1:2)
mm = t_str(3:4)
ss = t_str(5:6)
ms = t_str(7:10)
```

6 Add a conditional test to output the date in USA and European formats, according to the current timezone
```
if (tz(1:3) == '-04') then
    print '(A)', 'New York (Eastern Time)'
    print '(A)', 'Date: '//m//'-'//d//'-'//y
else if (tz(1:3) == '+01') then
    print '(A)', 'London (British Summer Time)'
    print '(A)', 'Date: '//d//'-'//m//'-'//y
end if
```

Beware

This example makes no allowance for changes to the UTC offset during periods of daylight saving, when New York (EDT) is UTC-05 and London (GMT) is UTC-00. The program could, of course, be extended to recognize these changes.

7 Finally, output the current time, then end the program
```
    print '(A)', 'Time: '//hh//':'//mm//':'//ss//ms
end program
```

8 Save the file named as **datetime.f90**, then compile and run the program to see the current date, time, and timezone

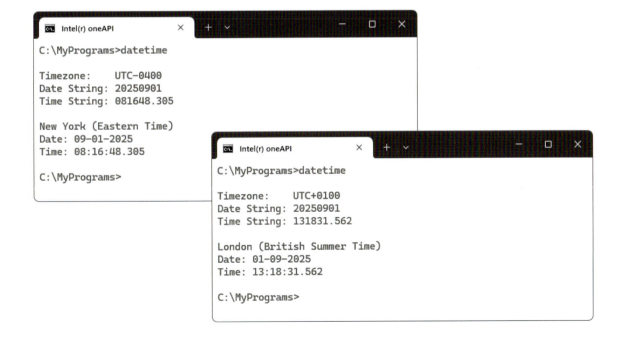

```
C:\MyPrograms>datetime

Timezone:    UTC-0400
Date String: 20250901
Time String: 081648.305

New York (Eastern Time)
Date: 09-01-2025
Time: 08:16:48.305

C:\MyPrograms>
```

```
C:\MyPrograms>datetime

Timezone:    UTC+0100
Date String: 20250901
Time String: 131831.562

London (British Summer Time)
Date: 01-09-2025
Time: 13:18:31.562

C:\MyPrograms>
```

Summary

- Strings are consecutive characters of a length specified by the **len** specifier in the **character** variable declaration.

- A **character** string variable can be allowed to resize by declaring it with the **allocatable** keyword.

- Memory space used by an **allocatable** variable must be freed by the **deallocate()** function.

- The **//** concatenation operator can be used to output multiple strings as a combined string.

- A substring can be specified in a **character** string by an extent specifier **(:)** stating its start and end index positions.

- A **character** string can be searched to see if it contains a specified substring by the **index()** function.

- The **len()** function returns the size of a **character** string variable, and the **len_trim()** function returns the string length.

- The **scan()** function and **verify()** function can be used to search a character string for a specified character set.

- The **trim()** function removes blank trailing spaces in output.

- The **adjustr()** and **adjustl()** functions can be used to shift a string within the **character** variable length.

- The **achar()** function returns an ASCII character, and the **iachar()** function returns a corresponding character code.

- The **repeat()** function returns multiple concatenated copies of a character or string.

- The **data_and_time()** function assigns the current date, time, and timezone to its specified variable arguments.

- Each component of date, time, and timezone can be assigned to individual variables using the **(:)** extent specifier.

5 Producing arrays

This chapter demonstrates how to manipulate data in Fortran array structures.

Declaring arrays

An array is a variable that can store multiple items of data – unlike a regular variable, which can only store one piece of data. The pieces of data are stored sequentially in array "elements" that are numbered in Fortran, starting at 1. So, the first value is stored in element 1, the second value is stored in element 2, etc. Array elements are identified by their "index" position in the array.

An array is declared in the same way as other variables, but additionally, the declaration must include a **dimension** keyword. This must be followed by **()** parentheses containing an integer that specifies how many elements the array should have. The syntax of an array declaration, therefore, looks like this:

> *data-type*, **dimension(** *number-of-elements* **) ::** *variable-name*

For example, the declaration of an array named "nums" to store six integer numbers looks like this:

> **integer, dimension(6) :: nums**

An individual element can be referenced by the array name followed by parentheses containing an element index number. For example, **nums(1)** references the first element in the example above. Similarly, the elements can be initialized by assigning values to individual elements, such as **nums(1)** = *value1*.

Alternatively, elements can be initialized efficiently by assigning values to individual elements in a loop:

> **do i = 1, 3**
> **   nums(i) =** *value*
> **end do**

There is also a shorthand option to initialize array elements using a comma-separated list of values within square brackets:

> **nums = [** *value1*, *value2*, *value3* **]**

Fortran provides three intrinsic functions that each accept the array name as their argument to describe the array structure:

- **rank()** – returns the number of dimensions.

- **shape()** – returns the number of elements in each dimension.

- **size()** – returns the total number of elements.

Don't forget

Fortran array index numbering starts at **1**, unlike other programming languages that begin array index numbering at **0**.

1 Begin a program that declares an integer array of three elements, plus an integer counter variable

```
program main
    implicit none
    integer(kind=2), dimension(3) :: arr
    integer(kind=1) :: i
```

array.f90

2 Next, initialize the elements individually, and output them

```
    arr(1) = 1
    arr(2) = 2
    arr(3) = 3
    print '(/,A,3I)', 'Array:', arr
```

3 Now, assign new values to the elements with a loop

```
    do i = 1, 3
        arr(i) = i * 10
    end do
    print '(/,A,3I)', 'Array:', arr
```

4 Then, use shorthand to assign new values to the elements

```
    arr = [100, 200, 300]
    print '(/,A,3I)', 'Array:', arr
```

5 Finally, output a description of the array structure

```
    print '(/,A,I6)', 'Rank - Number of dimensions:', rank(arr)
    print '(A,I3)', 'Shape - Elements per dimension:', shape(arr)
    print '(A,I5)', 'Size - Total no. of elements:', size(arr)
end program
```

6 Save the file named as **array.f90**, then compile and run the program to see the array element values and structure

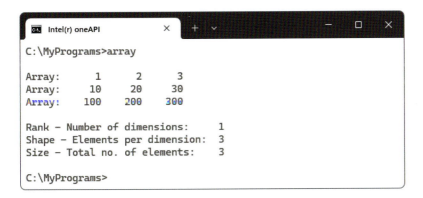

Addressing elements

Just as an extent specifier can be used to extract a substring from a string, an extent specifier can be used to extract a subset of elements from an array. In fact, a string can be regarded in many ways as an array of characters.

An array with a single dimension, like the array in the previous example, is known as a one-dimensional array or as a "flat" array:

Given the one-dimensional array above, containing eight elements, the elements can be addressed in several ways:

- **(n)** – addresses an individual element at position **n** within the array. For example, **(4)** addresses the fourth element (4).

- **(n1 : n2)** – addresses all elements within the array from **n1** to **n2** inclusive. For example, **(3:5)** addresses the third, fourth, and fifth elements (3,4,5).

Optionally, the extent specifier can omit the start or end element index number to address all elements up to, and including, the boundary element of the array:

- **(: n)** – addresses all elements from the first element in the array up to, and including, the element at position **n**. For example, an extent specifier **(:3)** addresses the first, second, and third elements (1,2,3).

- **(n :)** – addresses all elements from the element at position **n** up to, and including, the final element in the array. For example, an extent specifier **(6:)** addresses the sixth, seventh, and eighth elements (6,7,8).

Additionally, for one-dimensional arrays, the extent specifier can include a third argument to specify a "step" value to select every **n**th element in the array:

- **(n1 : n2 : n)** – addresses all **n**th elements within the array from **n1** to **n2** inclusive. For example, **(1:5:2)** addresses the first, third, and fifth elements (1,3,5).

...cont'd

1 Begin a program that declares an integer array of nine elements, plus an integer counter variable

```fortran
program main
    implicit none
    integer(kind=2), dimension(9) :: arr
    integer(kind=1) :: i
```

address.f90

2 Next, initialize the elements individually, and output them

```fortran
    do i = 1, 9
        arr(i) = i * 10
    end do
    print '(/,A,9I3)', 'Array:', arr
```

3 Now, output the value of a single element

```fortran
    print '(/,A,4X,I3)', 'Element 3:', arr(3)
```

4 Then, output a selection of array element values

```fortran
    print '(A,3I3)', 'Element 3 - 5 :', arr(3:5)
    print '(A,3I3)', 'Element 7 - | :', arr(7: )
    print '(A,3I3)', 'Element step 3:', arr(::3)
```

5 Finally, output a description of the array structure

```fortran
    print '(/,A,I6)', 'Rank - Number of dimensions:', rank(arr)
    print '(A,I3)', 'Shape - Elements per dimension:', shape(arr)
    print '(A,I5)', 'Size - Total no. of elements:', size(arr)
end program
```

6 Save the file named as **address.f90**, then compile and run the program to see the array element values and structure

```
Intel(r) oneAPI                    ×    +  ∨           —   □   ×

C:\MyPrograms>address

Array: 10 20 30 40 50 60 70 80 90

Element 3:     30
Element 3 - 5 : 30 40 50
Element 7 - | : 70 80 90
Element step 3: 10 40 70

Rank - Number of dimensions:      1
Shape - Elements per dimension:   9
Size - Total no. of elements:     9

C:\MyPrograms>
```

Declaring matrices

Fortran arrays can have more than a single dimension. In fact they can have up to seven dimensions according to the specifications.

An array with more than one dimension is known as a multi-dimensional array. Multi-dimensional arrays of three dimensions and more are less common, but a two-dimensional array – or "matrix" – is useful to store grid-based information, such as coordinates:

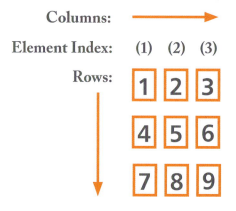

In Fortran, matrix elements are stored contiguously within memory in "column-major order". This means that each element of the first column is stored, before each element of the second column, and so on. For example, with the matrix above, the order in memory is (1, 4, 7) , (2, 5, 8) , (3, 6, 9) and, by default, will be output as such.

Elements of a matrix are referenced in a similar way to those in a flat one-dimensional array, but additionally specifying a column:

- (*n, c*) – addresses an individual element at index position *n* within column *c*. For example, **(2,2)** addresses the second element of the second column (5).

- (*n1 : n2, c*) – addresses all elements within the array from *n1* to *n2* inclusive, in column *c*. For example, **(1:2, 3)** addresses the first and second elements in the third column (3,6).

- (: *n, c*) – addresses all elements up to, and including element *n* in column *c*. For example, **(:2,1)** addresses the first and second elements in the first column (1,4).

Hot tip

Output in column-major order may not be desirable but examples later in this chapter demonstrate how the order can be changed.

...cont'd

1 Begin a program that declares a two-dimensional matrix of three rows and three columns, plus three counter variables

```fortran
program main
    implicit none
    integer(kind=1), dimension(3,3) :: mx
    integer(kind=1) :: i, j, k
```

matrix.f90

2 Next, add nested loops to initialize the matrix elements

```fortran
k = 0
do i = 1, 3
    do j = 1, 3
        k = k + 1
        mx(i, j) = k
    end do
end do
```

3 Now, output each row of the matrix

```fortran
print '(/,3I4)', mx(1:3,1)
print '(3I4)', mx(1:3,2)
print '(3I4)', mx(1:3,3)
```

4 Finally, output a description of the matrix structure

```fortran
print '(/,A,I5)', 'Rank  - Number of dimensions:', rank(mx)
print '(A,I3)', 'Shape - Elements per dimension:', shape(mx)
print '(A,I5)', 'Size - Total no. of elements:', size(mx)
print '(A,I3)', 'No. elements dimension 1:', size(mx, dim=1)
print '(A,I3)', 'No. elements dimension 2:', size(mx, dim=2)
end program
```

5 Save the file named as **matrix.f90**, then compile and run the program to see the matrix element values and structure

Notice how the **size()** function's **dim** attribute is used here to specify a dimension.

73

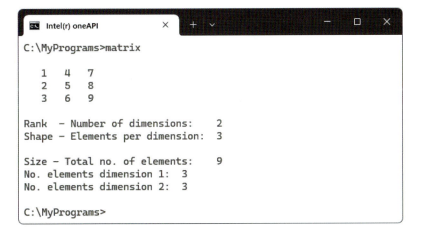

```
Intel(r) oneAPI                    ×    +  ∨          —   □   ×

C:\MyPrograms>matrix

    1    4    7
    2    5    8
    3    6    9

Rank  - Number of dimensions:    2
Shape - Elements per dimension:  3

Size - Total no. of elements:    9
No. elements dimension 1:  3
No. elements dimension 2:  3

C:\MyPrograms>
```

Reshaping arrays

The values in a one-dimensional flat array can be assigned to a matrix using the Fortran **reshape()** function. The **reshape()** function has this syntax:

matrix-variable = reshape(*array-variable*, shape, pad, order)

The **shape** argument is required and must be assigned a one-dimensional array that specifies the new shape. This must be an appropriate size to match the size of the array. For example, for a flat array size of 9, a **shape** of [3,3] would create an appropriate two-dimensional array also of size 9.

The **pad** argument is optional and can be used to provide additional elements to fill the matrix if necessary.

The **order** argument is optional but very useful to specify the element order by assigning a one-dimensional array. If omitted, the elements will be in row-major order. In a two-dimensional array, that **order** is [1,2] but assigning an **order** of [2,1] will place the elements in column-major order:

1 2 3 4 5 6 7 8

Given a flat one-dimensional array **arr** with eight elements, as above, the statement **reshape(arr, shape=[4,2])** produces a two-dimensional array with row-major order:

For the same one-dimensional array **arr** with eight elements as above, the statement **reshape(arr, shape=[4,2], order=[2,1])** produces a two-dimensional array with column-major order:

1 Begin a program that declares an array variable, a two-dimensional matrix variable, plus a counter variable

reshape.f90

```fortran
program main
    implicit none
    integer(kind=1), dimension(9) :: arr
    integer(kind=1), dimension(3,3) :: mx
    integer(kind=1) :: i
```

2 Next, add a loop to initialize the array elements and output their values

```fortran
    do i = 1, 9
        arr(i) = i * 10
    end do
    print '(/,A,9I4)', 'Array:', arr
```

3 Now, initialize the matrix and output the element values

```fortran
    mx = reshape(arr, shape=[3,3])
    print '(/,A)', 'Matrix Ordered by Row...'
    print '(3I8,/,3I8,/,3I8)', mx(1:3,1), mx(1:3,2), mx(1:3,3)
```

4 Then, change the element order and output their values

```fortran
    mx = reshape(arr, shape=[3,3], order=[2,1])
    print '(/,A)', 'Matrix Ordered by Column...'
    print '(3I8,/,3I8,/,3I8)', mx(1:3,1), mx(1:3,2), mx(1:3,3)
end program
```

5 Save the file named as **reshape.f90**, then compile and run the program to see the reshaped array element values

```
Intel(r) oneAPI              ×    +  ∨              —   □   ×

C:\MyPrograms>reshape

Array:  10  20  30  40  50  60  70  80  90

Matrix Ordered by Row...
        10        20        30
        40        50        60
        70        80        90

Matrix Ordered by Column...
        10        40        70
        20        50        80
        30        60        90

C:\MyPrograms>
```

Padding arrays

The values in two one-dimensional flat arrays can be assigned to a single matrix using the **pad** argument of the Fortran **reshape()** function. This can be assigned a second padding array variable to fill any empty elements if the matrix size is not completely filled by the first array variable.

The total number of array elements, calculated by adding the number of elements in the first array to the number of elements in the padding array, need not be identical to the total number of elements in the matrix:

● When the matrix elements are not completely filled by the first array, and the total number of array elements is <u>greater</u> than the total number of matrix elements, the empty matrix elements get filled by values taken from the padding array. This takes the required number of element values, starting from the first padding array element:

● When the matrix elements are not completely filled by the first array, and the total number of array elements is <u>less</u> that the total number of matrix elements, the empty matrix elements get filled by repeatedly taking values from the padding array:

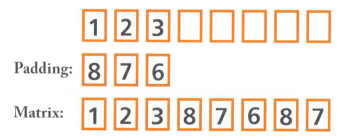

1 Begin a program that declares two array variables, a two-dimensional matrix variable, plus a counter variable

pad.f90

```fortran
program main
    implicit none
    integer(kind=1), dimension(9) :: arr
    integer(kind=1), dimension(8) :: padding
    integer(kind=1), dimension(3,5) :: mx
    integer(kind=1) :: i
```

2 Next, add loops to initialize the elements of both arrays, and output their values

```fortran
    do i = 1, 9
        arr(i) = i * 10
    end do
    print '(/,A,2X,9I4)', 'Array:', arr

    do i = 1, 8
        padding(i) = 90 - (i * 15)
    end do
    print '(A,8I4)', 'Padding:', padding
```

3 Then, initialize the matrix and output its element values

```fortran
    mx = reshape(arr, shape=[3,5], pad=padding)
    print '(/,A)', 'Padded and Ordered by Row:'
    do i = 1, 5
        print *, mx(1:3, i)
    end do
end program
```

4 Save the file named as **pad.f90**, then compile and run the program to see the matrix element values

```
C:\MyPrograms>pad

Array:    10  20  30  40  50  60  70  80  90
Padding:  75  60  45  30  15   0 -15 -30

Padded and Ordered by Row:
   10    20    30
   40    50    60
   70    80    90
   75    60    45
   30    15     0

C:\MyPrograms>
```

Intel(r) oneAPI

Transposing arrays

The rows and columns of a matrix can be swapped using the intrinsic Fortran **transpose()** function. This accepts the name of a matrix variable as its arguments, and assigns its result to another matrix variable. The matrix variables can have a different shape but must have the same total number of elements. For example, a matrix shaped 3x2 can be assigned to a matrix shaped 2x3 as they both have a total of six elements.

Fortran also provides two functions that allow rows and columns of a matrix to be manipulated by shifting their place in the matrix. The **eoshift()** "end-off" shift function moves the elements of a matrix along a specified dimension and has this syntax:

> **matrix2 = eoshift(*matrix1*, shift, boundary, dim)**

- The required **shift** argument specifies an integer of the amount by which to shift. This will shift left for positive integers and shift right for negative integers.

- The optional **boundary** argument can be used to specify a value to replace elements that have been shifted out. By default, if omitted, the replacement value is **0**.

- The optional **dim** argument specifies the dimension along which to shift. An assigned value of **1** (the default) shifts the columns, and a value of **2** shifts the rows.

The **cshift()** "circular" shift function also moves the elements of a matrix along a specified dimension, and has this syntax:

> **matrix2 = cshift(*matrix1*, shift, dim)**

- The required **shift** argument specifies an integer of the amount by which to shift. This will shift left for positive integers and shift right for negative integers. Unlike the **eoshift()** function, which replaces elements that have been shifted out with **0** or a specified boundary value, the **cshift()** function shifts in the element values it has just shifted out.

- The optional **dim** argument specifies the dimension along which to shift. An assigned value of **1** (the default) shifts the columns, and a value of **2** shifts the rows.

1
Begin a program that declares two matrix variables

```fortran
program main
    implicit none
    integer(kind=1), dimension(2,3) :: mx
    integer(kind=1), dimension(3,2) :: tmx
```

transpose.f90

2
Next, initialize and output the first matrix element values

```fortran
mx = reshape( [1,2,3,4,5,6], shape=[2,3] )
print '(/,A,/,2I8,/,2I8,/,2I8)', 'Matrix...', &
    mx(1:2,1), mx(1:2,2), mx(1:2,3)
```

3
Now, transpose the matrix, and output the new shape

```fortran
tmx = transpose(mx)
print '(A,/,3I8,/,3I8)', 'Transposed...', &
    tmx(1:3,1), tmx(1:3,2)
```

4
Then, shift the transposed matrix's columns left and right

```fortran
tmx = cshift(tmx, shift=1)
print '(A,/,3I8,/,3I8)', 'Circular Shift Left...', &
    tmx(1:3,1), tmx(1:3,2)

tmx = eoshift(tmx, shift=-1)
print '(A,/,3I8,/,3I8)', 'End-Off Shift Right...', &
    tmx(1:3,1), tmx(1:3,2
end program
```

5
Save the file named as **transpose.f90**, then compile and run the program to see the matrix element values

```
Intel(r) oneAPI

C:\MyPrograms>transpose

Matrix...
        1        2
        3        4
        5        6
Transposed...
        1        3        5
        2        4        6
Circular Shift Left...
        3        5        1
        4        6        2
End-Off Shift Right...
        0        3        5
        0        4        6

C:\MyPrograms>
```

Inspecting arrays

Fortran provides several intrinsic functions to allow inspection of the values within the elements of a matrix. These can accept a mask argument that can be an expression that evaluates to a logical true or false, or numerical **0** (false) or **-1** (true).

Reduction Functions

● **all(*mask, dim*)** – returns a logical value of true if <u>all</u> elements match the logical **mask** value. The optional **dim** argument can specify the dimension to inspect.

● **any(*mask, dim*)** – returns a logical value of true if <u>any</u> elements match the logical **mask** value. The optional **dim** argument can specify the dimension to inspect.

● **count(*mask, dim*)** – returns a numerical value that is the number of elements that match the logical **mask** value. The optional **dim** argument can specify the dimension to inspect.

● **maxval(*matrix-variable, dim, mask*)** – returns the <u>largest</u> value in the matrix. The optional **dim** argument can specify the dimension to inspect. The optional **mask** argument can specify a logical value to match.

● **minval(*matrix-variable, dim, mask*)** – returns the <u>smallest</u> value in the matrix. The optional **dim** argument can specify the dimension to inspect. The optional **mask** argument can specify a logical value to match.

● **sum(*matrix-variable, dim, mask*)** – returns the sum total value of all elements in the matrix. The optional **dim** argument can specify the dimension to inspect. The optional **mask** argument can specify a logical value to match.

Location Functions

● **maxloc(*matrix-variable, mask*)** – returns the position of the <u>largest</u> value in the matrix. The optional **mask** argument can specify a logical value to match.

● **minloc(*matrix-variable, mask*)** – returns the position of the <u>smallest</u> value in the matrix. The optional **mask** argument can specify a logical value to match.

1 Begin a program that declares a matrix variable

```fortran
program main
    implicit none
    integer(kind=2), dimension(3,3) :: mx
```

2 Next, initialize the matrix and output its element values

```fortran
mx = reshape([75,32,18,91,5,8,53,88,71], shape=[3,3])
print '(/,A)','Matrix...'
print '(3I4)', mx(1:3,1), mx(1:3,2), mx(1:3,3)
```

3 Now, add statements to output the result of logical tests

```fortran
print '(/,A)', 'Logical Tests...'
print '(A,3X,3L)', 'All Row Values Above 50:', all(mx > 50, 1)
print '(A,3L)', 'All Column Values Above 50:', all(mx > 50, 2)
print '(A,7X,L)', 'Any Values Above 90:', any(mx > 90)
```

4 Then, add statements to output the result of numerical tests

```fortran
print '(/,A)', 'Numerical Tests...'
print '(A,I2)', 'No. of Values Above 50:', count(mx > 50)
print '(A,I3,1X,A,I2,I2)', 'Maximum Value:', &
    maxval(mx), 'at (column,row):', maxloc(mx)
print '(A,I3,1X,A,I2,I2)', 'Minimum Value:', &
    minval(mx), 'at (column,row):', minloc(mx)
print '(A,I4)', 'Sum of All Values:', sum(mx)
end program
```

5 Save the file named as **inspect.f90**, then compile and run the program to see the matrix inspection results

```
Intel(r) oneAPI              ×    +  ⌄              —  □  ×

C:\MyPrograms>inspect

Matrix...
  75  32  18
  91   5   8
  53  88  71
Logical Tests...
All Row Values Above 50:     F F T
All Column Values Above 50: T F F
Any Values Above 90:         T

Numerical Tests...
No. of Values Above 50: 5
Maximum Value: 91 at (column,row): 1 2
Minimum Value:  5 at (column,row): 2 2
Sum of All Values: 441

C:\MyPrograms>
```

Masking arrays

A matrix mask in Fortran can be created as a matrix of the same size and shape as an initial matrix. Each element in the mask should contain an expression that can evaluate to true or false, or the numerical logical equivalents of **0** (false) or **-1** (true).

Comparing the mask elements with those of the elements in the original matrix can filter the elements to exclude all element values where its equivalent mask element is false. Typically, the excluded elements can then be assigned a zero value **0**.

The Fortran **product()** function can usefully return the multiplied product of all elements in the filtered matrix, and has this syntax:

> product(*matrix-variable*, dim=*dimension*, mask=*mask-matrix*)

Where the **dim** argument is assigned a value of **1**, the function will return the product of all row element values, and when assigned a value of **2**, it will return the product of all column element values.

mask.f90

1 Begin a program that declares two matrix variables, plus two counter variables

```
program main
    implicit none
    integer(kind=2), dimension(3,3) :: mx
    logical, dimension(3,3) :: net
    integer(kind=1) :: i, j
```

2 Also, declare an array to store product results

```
    integer(kind=2), dimension(3) :: prod
```

3 Next, initialize both matrix variables

```
    mx = reshape( [1,2,3,4,5,6,7,8,9], shape=[3,3] )
    net = reshape( [0,-1,-1,0,1,-1,-1,0,-1], shape=[3,3] )
```

4 Now, output the numerical element values in the original matrix

```
    print '(/,A)', 'Matrix...'
    print '(3I4)', mx(1:3,1), mx(1:3,2), mx(1:3,3)
```

5 Then, output the logical element values in the mask matrix

```
    print '(/,A)', 'Mask...'
    print '(3I4)', net(1:3,1), net(1:3,2), net(1:3,3)
```

6 Add nested loops to identify all elements in the original matrix where the equivalent element in the mask is false

```fortran
do i = 1, 3
    do j = 1, 3
        if (net(i, j) /= .true.) then
            mx(i, j) = 0
        end if
    end do
end do
```

7 Now, output the element values in the filtered matrix

```fortran
print '(/,A)', 'Matrix True Values...'
print '(3I4)', mx(1:3,1), mx(1:3,2), mx(1:3,3)
```

8 Finally, output the products of filtered rows and columns

```fortran
prod = product(mx, dim=1, mask=net)
print '(/,A,3X,3I5)', &
    'Product Dimension1 (Row Where True):', prod
prod = product(mx, dim=2, mask=net)
print '(A,3I5)', &
    'Product Dimension2 (Column Where True):', prod
```

9 Save the file named as **mask.f90**, then compile and run the program to see the filtered matrix results

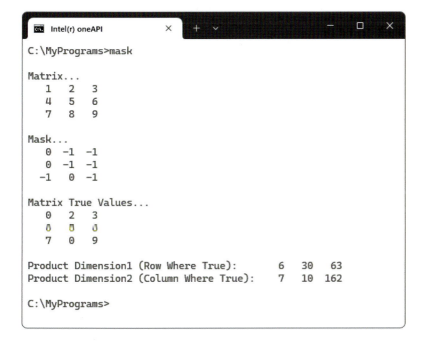

```
Intel(r) oneAPI

C:\MyPrograms>mask

Matrix...
    1   2   3
    4   5   6
    7   8   9

Mask...
    0  -1  -1
    0  -1  -1
   -1   0  -1

Matrix True Values...
    0   2   3
    0   0   0
    7   0   9

Product Dimension1 (Row Where True):     6   30   63
Product Dimension2 (Column Where True):  7   10  162

C:\MyPrograms>
```

Hot tip

Row products are:
2 x 3 = 6
5 x 6 = 30
7 x 9 = 63
Column products are:
7 = 7
2 x 5 = 10
3 x 6 x 9 = 162

Constructing arrays

Fortran provides a number of construction functions that can be used to manipulate matrix elements:

- **merge()** – combines two arrays of the same size and shape based upon a mask that must also be of the same size and shape. The **merge()** function has this syntax:

> **merge(*matrix1-variable, matrix2-variable, mask-matrix*)**

The function returns elements of the first matrix where the corresponding mask element is true, and returns elements of the second matrix where the mask element is false.

- **pack()** – returns an array of element values based upon a mask, and has this syntax:

> **pack(*matrix-variable, mask-matrix*)**

The function returns elements of the matrix where the corresponding mask element is true.

- **spread()** – replicates elements along a specified dimension, making a specified number of copies, with this syntax:

> **spread(*array-variable*, dim=*dimension* ncopies=*n*)**

The function expands the element array along the specified dimension to accommodate the copied elements.

construct.f90

1 Begin a program that declares four matrix variables and one array variable

```
program main
  implicit none
  integer(kind=1), dimension(2,3) :: positive, negative, blend
  logical, dimension(2,3) :: net
  integer(kind=1), dimension(4) :: packed
```

2 Next, initialize three matrix variables

```
positive = reshape( [1,2,3,4,5,6], shape=[2,3] )
negative = reshape( [-1,-2,-3,-4,-5,-6], shape=[2,3] )
net = reshape( [-1,-1,0,-1,-1,0], shape=[2,3] )
```

3 Now, output the element values of all three matrix variables

```
print '(/,A,1X,6I5)', 'Positive Matrix:', positive
print '(A,1X,6I5)', 'Negative Matrix:', negative
print '(A,5X,6L5)', 'Mask Matrix:',net
```

4 Then, merge all three matrix variables to initialize the fourth matrix variable and output the merged element values

```
blend = merge(positive, negative, net)
print '(/,A,3X,6I5)', 'Merged Matrix:', blend
```

5 Initialize the array variable with all true element values of the merged matrix

```
packed = pack(positive, net)
print '(/,A,3X,6I5)', 'True Elements:', packed
```

6 Finally, output replicated copies of two elements in each dimension

```
print '(/,A,4X,5I5)', 'Spread Dim 1:',  &
    spread( packed(1:2), dim=1, ncopies=2)

print '(A,4X,5I5)', 'Spread Dim 2:', &
    spread( packed(1:2), dim=2, ncopies=2)
end program
```

7 Save the file named as **construct.f90**, then compile and run the program to see the constructed results

```
 Intel(r) oneAPI          ×   + ∨              —  □  ×

C:\MyPrograms>construct

Positive Matrix:    1    2    3    4    5    6
Negative Matrix:   -1   -2   -3   -4   -5   -6
Mask Matrix:        T    T    F    T    T    F

Merged Matrix:      1    2   -3    4    5   -6

True Elements:      1    2    4    5

Spread Dim 1:       1    1    2    2
Spread Dim 2:       1    2    1    2

C:\MyPrograms>
```

Multiplying arrays

Fortran provides two functions that can be used to multiply the element values of arrays and matrices to compute their product – most useful in linear algebra and scientific computing.

- **dot_product()** – for array elements containing numeric values, this function multiplies corresponding elements in two arrays to compute their products and returns the sum of all products. The function has this syntax:

> **dot_product(*array-variable1, array-variable2*)**

For array elements containing logical values, this function returns true if any corresponding elements are both true.

- **matmul()** – multiplies elements in two matrices to compute their products and returns the sum of all products. The number of columns in the first matrix must equal the number of columns in the second matrix. The function has this syntax:

> **matmul(*matrix-variable1, matrix-variable2*)**

The function returns a matrix whose elements contain the sum of multiplying the two matrix's elements.

multiply.f90

1 Begin a program that declares two array variables and three matrix variables

```
program main
    implicit none
    integer(kind=1), dimension(3) :: x, y
    integer(kind=1), dimension(2,2) :: a, b, c
```

2 Next, initialize the arrays and output their element values

```
x = [1,2,3]
y = [4,5,6]
print '(/,A,/,3I5,/,3I5)', 'Arrays...', x, y
```

3 Now, output the dot product sum of multiplying the array elements, and an explanation of the operation

```
print '(/,A,I5)', 'Array Product:', dot_product(x,y)

print '(A,I2,A,I1,A2,I2,A,I1,A2,I2,A,I1)', 'Steps:', &
    x(1), '*', y(1), '+', x(2), '*', y(2), '+', x(3), '*', y(3)
```

...cont'd

4 Initialize two matrices and output their element values
```
a = reshape( [2,1,3,4], shape=[2,2])
b = reshape( [5,6,7,8], shape=[2,2])
print '(/,A,/,2I5,/,2I5)', 'Matrix a...', a
print '(/,A,/,2I5,/,2I5)', 'Matrix b...', b
```

5 Then, output the product sum of multiplying the matrix elements, and an explanation of the operation
```
c = matmul(a,b)
print '(/,A,4I5)', 'Matrix Product:', c(1:2,1), c(1:2,2)

print '(A,I2,A,I1,A2,I2,A,I1)', 'Steps:', &
    a(1,1), '*', b(2,1), '+', a(1,1), '*', b(2,2)
print '(6X,I2,A,I1,A2,I2,A,I1)', &
    a(1,2), '*', b(1,1), '+', a(1,1), '*', b(1,2)
print '(6X,I2,A,I1,A2,I2,A,I1)', &
    a(2,1), '*', b(2,1), '+', a(2,2), '*', b(2,2)
print '(6X,I2,A,I1,A2,I2,A,I1)', &
    a(1,2), '*', b(1,1), '+', a(2,2), '*', b(2,1)
end program
```

6 Save the file named as **multiply.f90**, then compile and run the program to see the multiplied product sums

```
C:\MyPrograms>multiply

Arrays...
    1    2    3
    4    5    6

Array Product:    32
Steps: 1*4 + 2*5 + 3*6

Matrix a...
    2    1
    3    4

Matrix b...
    5    6
    7    8

Matrix Product:   28   29   38   39
Steps: 2*6 + 2*8
       3*5 + 2*7
       1*6 + 4*8
       3*5 + 4*6

C:\MyPrograms>
```

Resizing arrays

Declaring numeric array variables of a specified length allows the program to assign new values to their elements as the program proceeds, providing the total length of the array remains the same size as specified in its declaration.

Usefully, a numeric array variable can be allowed to resize as the program proceeds by declaring it with the **allocatable** keyword. The dimension must then be specified by a : lone colon character to indicate that its length can be varied. The syntax of resizable numeric array variables looks like this:

> **integer(kind=***n***), dimension(:), allocatable ::** *variable-name*
> **real(kind=***n***), dimension(:), allocatable ::** *variable-name*

When the program no longer needs an **allocatable** variable, its memory space must be freed by specifying the variable name to an intrinsic **deallocate()** function. Multiple variable names can be specified as arguments to this function in a comma-separated list:

> **deallocate(** *variable-name1***,** *variable-name2* **)**

The current status of an array variable can be found by specifying the variable name as the argument to the intrinsic **allocated()** function to return a logical true or false status value.

The largest number ("upper bound") that can be used to index a particular dimension of an array variable can be revealed using the intrinsic **ubound()** function with this syntax:

> **ubound(** *array-variable***, dim=***dimension***, kind=***kind* **)**

The **dim** argument is optional but can be included to specify the dimension to query when the array has multiple dimensions. The **kind** argument is also optional but can be included to specify the kind of the returned numeric value.

There is also a companion **lbound()** function that can reveal the smallest number ("lower bound") that can be used to index a particular dimension of an array variable. The syntax of the **lbound()** function looks and performs like that of the **ubound()** function:

> **lbound(** *array-variable***, dim=***dimension***, kind=***kind* **)**

The **ubound()** and **lbound()** functions are useful for handling arrays when their bounds are not fixed.

1 Begin a program that declares a resizable integer array
```fortran
program main
    implicit none
    integer(kind=1), dimension(:), allocatable :: arr
```

allocate.f90

2 Next, initialize the array and confirm it has been allocated memory space
```fortran
    print '(/,A,L)', 'Allocated?:', allocated(arr)
    arr = [1,2,3,4,5,6,7,8]
    print '(A,L)', 'Allocated?:', allocated(arr)
```

3 Now, output the array values and bounds
```fortran
    print '(/,A,8I4)', 'Initialized Array:', arr
    print '(A,I1,A3,I2)', 'Bounds:', lbound(arr), 'to', ubound(arr)
```

4 Assign a larger array to the array variable, then output its new values and bounds
```fortran
    arr = [10,20,30,40,50,60,70,80,90,100]
    print '(/,A,10I4)', 'Reassigned Array:', arr
    print '(A,I1,A3,I3)', 'Bounds:', lbound(arr), 'to', ubound(arr)
```

5 Finally, free the allocated memory space
```fortran
    deallocate(arr)
    print '(/,A,L)', 'Allocated?:', allocated(arr)
end program
```

6 Save the file named as **allocate.f90**, then compile and run the program to see the resizable array

```
Intel(r) oneAPI                    ×    +  ∨              —  □  ×

C:\MyPrograms>allocate

Allocated?: F
Allocated?: T

Initialized Array:   1   2   3   4   5   6   7   8
Bounds:1 to 8

Reassigned Array:  10  20  30  40  50  60  70  80  90 100
Bounds:1 to 10

Allocated?: F

C:\MyPrograms>
```

Resizing matrices

Declaring numeric matrix variables of specified length dimensions allows the program to assign new values to their elements as the program proceeds, providing the total length of the matrix dimensions remains the same size as specified in its declaration.

Usefully, a numeric matrix variable can be allowed to dynamically resize as the program proceeds by declaring it with the **allocatable** keyword. The dimensions must be specified by a : colon character for each dimension to indicate that its length can be varied. The syntax of resizable two-dimensional matrix variables looks like this:

> **integer(kind=*n*), dimension(: , :), allocatable :: *variable-name***
> **real(kind=*n*), dimension(: , :), allocatable :: *variable-name***

When the program no longer needs an **allocatable** variable, its memory space must be freed by specifying the variable name to an intrinsic **deallocate()** function. Multiple variable names can be specified as arguments to this function in a comma-separated list:

> **deallocate(*variable-name1*, *variable-name2*)**

The current status of a matrix variable can be found by specifying the variable name as the argument to the intrinsic **allocated()** function to return a logical true or false status value.

The largest possible index ("upper bound") in each dimension of a matrix can be revealed using the intrinsic **ubound()** function with this syntax:

> **ubound(*array-variable*, dim=*dimension*, kind=*kind*)**

The **dim** argument is optional but if omitted the **ubound()** function will return the upper bound value in all dimensions. The **dim** argument can be used to specify the dimension to query. The **kind** argument is also optional but can be included to specify the kind of the returned numeric value.

The companion **lbound()** function can reveal the smallest possible index ("lower bound") in each dimension of a matrix variable. The syntax of the **lbound()** function looks and performs like that of the **ubound()** function.

1 Begin a program that declares a resizable integer matrix

```fortran
program main
    implicit none
    integer(kind=1), dimension( : , : ), allocatable :: mx
```

dynamic.f90

2 Next, initialize the matrix, then display its memory status, element values, and the bounds of its second dimension

```fortran
mx = reshape( [1,2,3,4,5,6], shape=[3,2], order=[2,1] )
print '(/,A,L)', 'Allocated?:', allocated(mx)
print '(A,/,3I5,/,3I5)', 'Matrix...', mx(1:3,1), mx(1:3,2)
print '(A,I3,A3,I3)', 'Bounds Dim 2:', &
    lbound(mx, dim=2), 'to', ubound(mx, dim=2)
```

3 Assign a larger matrix to the matrix variable, then output its new values and the bounds of its first dimension

```fortran
mx = reshape( [1,2,3,4,5,6,7,8,9,10], &
    shape=[5,2], order=[1,2] )
print '(/,A,/,5I5,/,5I5)', 'Reassigned Matrix...', &
    mx(1:5,1), mx(1:5,2)
print '(A,I3,A3,I3)', 'Bounds Dim 1:', &
    lbound(mx, dim=1), 'to', ubound(mx, dim=1)
```

4 Finally, free the allocated memory space

```fortran
deallocate(mx)
print '(A,L)', 'Allocated?:', allocated(mx)
end program
```

5 Save the file named as **dynamic.f90**, then compile and run the program to see the dynamically resizable matrix

```
Intel(r) oneAPI                        ×    +  ⌄    —   □   ×

C:\MyPrograms>dynamic

Allocated?: T
Matrix...
    1    3    5
    2    4    6
Bounds Dim 2:  1 to  2

Reassigned Matrix...
    1    2    3    4    5
    6    7    8    9   10
Bounds Dim 1:  1 to  5
Allocated?: F

C:\MyPrograms>
```

Summary

- An array is a variable that can store multiple items of data.

- The **rank()**, **shape()**, and **size()** functions describe array structure.

- Array elements can be addressed individually or by an **(:)** extent specifier, which may optionally specify a step value.

- An array with more than one dimension is known as a multi-dimensional array. A two-dimensional array is called a matrix.

- The values in a one-dimensional flat array can be assigned to a matrix using the **reshape()** function.

- A padding array can fill all empty elements of a matrix.

- The rows and columns of a matrix can be swapped using the intrinsic **transpose()** function.

- Rows and columns of a matrix can be manipulated by shifting their place in the matrix by **eoshift()** and **cshift()** functions.

- Arrays can be inspected by **all()**, **any()**, **count()**, **maxval()**, **minval()**, **sum()**, **maxloc()**, and **minloc()** functions.

- A matrix mask is a matrix of true and false values, and is the same size and shape as an initial matrix.

- The construction functions **merge()**, **pack()**, and **spread()** can be used to manipulate matrix elements.

- The **dot_product()** function multiplies corresponding elements in two arrays and returns the sum of all products.

- The **matmul()** function produces the matrix that is the result of standard matrix multiplication of two matrices.

- An array variable can be allowed to resize by declaring its dimension as **(:)** and by adding the **allocatable** keyword.

- When a program no longer needs an **allocatable** variable, its memory space must be freed by the **deallocate()** function.

- The largest and smallest indices in an array dimension can be found using the **ubound()** and **lbound()** functions.

- A two-dimensional matrix can be resizable by declaring its dimensions as **(: , :)** and by adding the **allocatable** keyword.

6

Managing input/output

This chapter demonstrates how Fortran can store and retrieve data in text files.

Reading input

Input from the user can be imported into a Fortran program and be assigned to a variable so that input can be used in the program. Text input from the standard input device (**stdin**) – typically, the keyboard – can usefully be assigned to a resizable character variable. The declaration of a resizable character variable must include the **allocatable** keyword. It differs slightly from the declaration of a resizable array, however, as the **character** keyword should be followed by (:) to indicate that its length can be varied. The syntax of resizable character array variable looks like this:

> **character(:), allocatable :: *variable-name***

Before assignments can be made to a resizable character variable, the program must first reserve sufficient memory space using an intrinsic **allocate()** function. This function must specify the data type, memory size requirement, and variable name as its arguments with this syntax:

> **allocate(*data-type*(*memory-size*) :: *variable-name*)**

When the program no longer needs an **allocatable** variable, its memory space must be freed by specifying the variable name to an intrinsic **deallocate()** function. Multiple variable names can be specified as arguments to this function in a comma-separated list:

> **deallocate(*variable-name1, variable-name2*)**

The current size of an allocatable variable can be found by specifying its name as the argument to the intrinsic **len()** function.

User input can be imported into a program and be assigned to a variable by a **read()** function. This can also assign a space-separated list of text strings to multiple variables with this syntax:

> **read(*,*) *variable-name1, variable-name2***

The size of the text strings input by the user may not completely fill the allocated number of memory spaces, so the empty blank trailing spaces should be removed by the intrinsic **trim()** function. For example:

> ***variable-name* = trim(*variable-name*)**

The trimmed text strings can then easily be used in output responses to the user.

1 Begin a program that declares two resizable character variables

```fortran
program main
    implicit none
    character(:), allocatable :: str1, str2
```

F
input.f90

2 Allocate to each variable memory space for 16 characters

```fortran
allocate(character(16) :: str1, str2)
```

3 Next, request user input to initialize the character variables

```fortran
print '(/,A)', 'Enter Your First & Last Name...'
read(*,*) str1, str2
```

4 Now, output the initial allocated memory size

```fortran
print '(/,A,3X,2I4)', 'Size Allocated:', len(str1), len(str2)
```

5 Then, reduce the memory requirement to suit the character length of the user input and output the size

```fortran
str1 = trim(str1)
str2 = trim(str2)
print '(A,2I4)', 'Size When Trimmed:', len(str1), len(str2)
```

6 Output responses to the user, then free the memory space

```fortran
print '(A)', 'Welcome, '//str1//' '//str2
print '(3A)', 'Have a great day, ', str1, '!'
deallocate(str1, str2)
end program
```

7 Save the file named as **input.f90**, then compile and run the program to see the input responses

```
Intel(r) oneAPI                    ×    + ∨      —  □  ×

C:\MyPrograms>input

Enter Your First & Last Name...
Sally Jones

Size Allocated:    16  16
Size When Trimmed:  5   5
Welcome, Sally Jones
Have a great day, Sally!

C:\MyPrograms>
```

Writing output

The Fortran **print** * statement provides a simple way to display output on the standard output device (**stdout**), typically the screen:

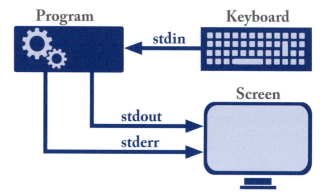

More flexibility is provided by the intrinsic **write()** function. This allows the program to output to the screen or to a file. It has many possible attributes but its common form has this syntax:

> **write(unit=***unit-specifier*,
> **fmt=***format-specifier*,
> **advance=***advance-specifier*) *string-to-output*

- The unit specifier is required but can simply be assigned an * asterisk character to denote that the standard output device should be used. Optionally, the **unit=** part can be omitted.

- The format specifier is required and can be a string list of edit descriptors, as used with the print statement in previous examples, or can be assigned an * asterisk character to denote that the default format should be used. Optionally, the **fmt=** part can be omitted.

- The advance specifier is optional and determines whether the output should add a final newline. It can be assigned a string value of **'no'** to inhibit the newline or **'yes'** to allow the newline. The default value is **'yes'** to allow the newline.

The shortest version of the **write()** function's syntax looks like this:

> **write(*, *)** *string-to-output*

It is useful to include the advance specifier with a **'no'** value when requesting user input so that the prompt remains on the same line as the request string.

1 Begin a program that declares a resizable character variable and a real number variable

```
program main
    implicit none
    character(:), allocatable :: uname
    real :: amount
```

response.f90

2 Allocate variable memory space for 16 characters

```
    allocate(character(16) :: uname)
```

3 Request text input and assign it to the character variable

```
    write(*, fmt='(/,A)', advance='no') 'Enter your name:'
    read(*,*) uname
```

4 Trim the input, then output it in a concatenated response

```
    uname = trim(uname)
    write(*, fmt='(A)') 'Thanks, '//uname
```

5 Request numeric input and assign it to the real variable

```
    write(*, fmt='(/,A)', advance='no') &
        'Now enter any amount:'
    read(*,*) amount
```

6 Output the user input in a formatted response, then free the memory space

```
    write(*, fmt='(A,F5.2)')  'Amount is:', amount
    deallocate(uname)
end program
```

7 Save the file named as **response.f90**, then compile and run the program to see the output responses

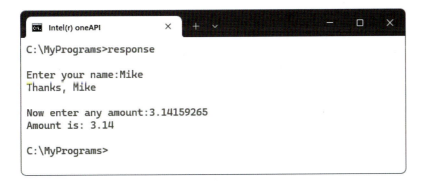

```
Intel(r) oneAPI

C:\MyPrograms>response

Enter your name:Mike
Thanks, Mike

Now enter any amount:3.14159265
Amount is: 3.14

C:\MyPrograms>
```

Writing files

The **write()** function can be used to create a text file and write data into a text file of a specified file name. Before attempting to create a new file, the intrinsic Fortran **inquire()** function can be used to see if a file of the specified name already exists. This function accepts two arguments to specify the file name, and a variable to receive a true or false result, with this syntax:

> **inquire(file=***filename*, exist=*exist-variable* **)**

The value assigned to the specified variable can then be tested to determine its Boolean value. If the file name does not already exist, a new file of that name can be created by the **open()** function, which has this basic syntax:

> **open(unit=***unit-specifier*, file=*filename*, status='new' **)**

The unit specifier must specify a unit number for the file, and this must be unique within the program. This can be manually assigned as an integer but to be sure of avoiding conflicts, Fortran can automatically assign an unused unit number to a **newunit** argument, in place of the **unit** argument, with this syntax:

> **open(newunit=***unit-variable*, file=*filename*, status='new' **)**

The variable assigned to the **newunit** argument will then store the unique unit number, which can be used to reference the file throughout the program.

Once the new file has been successfully opened, the **write()** function can then write data into the file by specifying its unit number and format, using this syntax:

> **write(unit=***unit-variable*, fmt=*format-specifier* **)**

After writing data into the opened file, the file should then be closed by specifying its unit number as the argument to the intrinsic **close()** function, with this syntax:

> **close(*unit-variable*)**

It is important to close the file to ensure the data is properly written and resources are released.

1 Begin a program that declares a constant and three variables

write.f90

```fortran
program main.
    implicit none
    character(len=8), parameter :: FILENAME = 'data.dat'
    logical :: found
    integer(kind=1) :: i, unit_num
```

2 Next, check to see if the file already exists

```fortran
    inquire(file=FILENAME, exist=found)
    if (found) then
        print '(/,A,1X,A,1X,A)', 'File:', FILENAME, 'already exists!'
    else
```

3 Otherwise, create a new file and write data into it

```fortran
        open(newunit=unit_num, file=FILENAME, status='new')
        write(unit=unit_num, fmt='(A,/)') 'Counting Up...'
        do i = 1, 10
            write(unit=unit_num, fmt='(I4)', advance='no') i
        end do
```

4 Now, close the file and output a confirmation message

```fortran
        close(unit_num)
        print '(/,A,1X,A,1X,A)', 'File:', FILENAME, 'data written.'
    end if
end program
```

5 Save the file named as **write.f90**, then compile and run the program to see the new file created

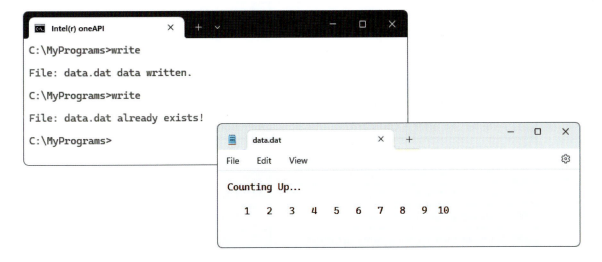

Appending data

The process to append data to an existing file is similar to the process of creating a new file – except the status should now be specified as 'old' and a **position** argument must be specified as 'append' in order to set the position at the end of the file. Additionally, the **open()** function can include an **iostat** argument to capture the status of the input/output (io) operation:

> open(newunit=*unit-variable*, file=*filename*,
>   status='old', position='append' iostat=*io-variable*)

The **iostat** argument is assigned an integer variable to store the io status. If there are no errors, the status is **0**, otherwise, an error code is returned. Some common error codes are listed below:

Error Code Table			
-1	End of file	21	Zero raised to zero power
-2	End of record	22	Floating point division by zero
0	No error	23	Floating point arithmetic underflow
1	Floating point arithmetic overflow	24	Compilation not by profile
2	Integer arithmetic overflow	27	Invalid floating point number
3	Character outside range 0-255	28	Negative argument to square root
4	Argument/function name wrong length	29	Call to missing routine
6	Inconsistent call to routine	30	Storage heap is corrupt
7	Do loop has no increment	31	Float too big for integer conversion
8	User-specified range check error	32	Second argument to MOD is zero
9	Array bound error	37	Integer divide overflow
10	Lower substring > upper	38	Illegal character assignment
11	Array subscript out of range	43	Invalid command
12	Lower substring out of range	44	Unable to open file
13	Illegal character assignment	45	String not found
14	Attempt to alter a constant	46	Routine not found
15	Attempt to access undefined argument	47	Invalid expression
16	Lower array bound > upper	50	Undefined input/output error
17	Upper substring out of range	51	Format/data mismatch
18	Routine entered recursively	52	Invalid character in field
19	Array argument < dummy argument	53	Input/output overflow

...cont'd

1 Begin a program that declares a constant and three variables

```fortran
program main
    implicit none
    character(len=8), parameter :: FILENAME = 'data.dat'
    integer(kind=1) :: i, unit_num, ios
```

append.f90

2 Next, attempt to open an existing file to append data

```fortran
open(newunit=unit_num, file=FILENAME, &
    status='old', position='append', iostat=ios)
```

3 Test the io status and output a message if an error occurs

```fortran
if (ios /= 0) then
    write(0, '(A,I4)') 'Error: File not found. IOSTAT=', ios
```

4 Otherwise, append data to the existing file

```fortran
else
    do i = 11, 20
        write(unit=unit_num, fmt='(I4)', advance='no') i
    end do
```

5 Now, close the file and output a confirmation message

```fortran
    close(unit_num)
    write(*, '(/,A,A)') 'Data appended to:', FILENAME
end if
end program
```

6 Save the file named as **append.f90**, then compile and run the program to see data appended to an existing file

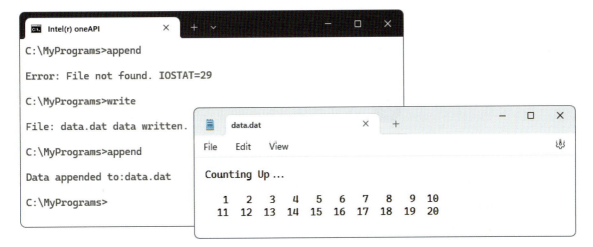

Reading files

The Fortran intrinsic **read()** function can be used to read data from text files into a receiving variable with this syntax:

> read(*unit-variable*, fmt=*format-specifier*,
> iostat=*io-variable*) *receiving-variable-name*

The unit variable can be the unique number assigned by the **newunit** argument in the **open()** function, in the same way as with the **write()** function.

The format specifier can specify a particular data format to read. For example, **fmt='(A16)'** will only read character string data of 16 characters in length. Conversely, the * wildcard character can be specified to read all data.

The **iostat** argument of the **read()** function can be tested for a **0** zero value to see if any errors have occurred when attempting to read from a file. If an error does occur, the test can output an error message and quit the program using the Fortran **stop** keyword.

The **iostat** argument of the **read()** function can also be tested for a **-1** value to see if the end of the file has been reached. If the end of the file has been reached, the test can close the file by specifying the unit variable as the argument to the **close()** function.

For confirmation that the data has been successfully retrieved, the **write()** function can output the data from the receiving variables.

read.f90

1. Begin a program that declares a constant and five variables

```fortran
program main
   implicit none
   character(len=8), parameter :: FILENAME = 'data.dat'
   integer(kind=1) : : i, unit_num, ios
   integer(kind=1), dimension(20) :: nums
   character(len=16) :: str
```

2. Next, attempt to open an existing file to read data, or report an error and stop the program

```fortran
open(newunit=unit_num, file=FILENAME, &
     status='old', iostat=ios)
if (ios /= 0) then
   write(0, '(/,A,I2)') 'Error: File not found. IOSTAT=', ios
   stop
end if
```

3 Now, read formatted character data, or report an error and stop the program

```
read(unit_num, fmt='(A16)', iostat=ios) str
if (ios /= 0) then
    write(0, '(/,A,I2)') 'Error: IOSTAT=', ios
    stop
end if
```

4 Then, read all other data and close the file when the end of the file is reached

```
read(unit_num, fmt=*, iostat=ios) nums
if (ios == -1) then
    close(unit_num)
end if
```

5 Finally, output the string and integer data read from the file into variables

```
write(*, fmt='(/,A16)' ) str
write(*, fmt='(/,10I4, /, 10I4)' ) nums
end program
```

6 Save the file named as **read.f90**, then compile and run the program to see the data read from an existing file

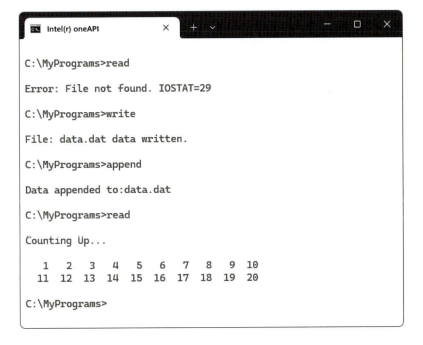

```
C:\MyPrograms>read

Error: File not found. IOSTAT=29

C:\MyPrograms>write

File: data.dat data written.

C:\MyPrograms>append

Data appended to:data.dat

C:\MyPrograms>read

Counting Up...

  1   2   3   4   5   6   7   8   9  10
 11  12  13  14  15  16  17  18  19  20

C:\MyPrograms>
```

Scratching files

Fortran offers the ability to create a temporary "scratch" file that is created during execution of a program then automatically deleted when the program ends. Scratch files are unnamed so that the programmer cannot specify a file name or path. A temporary file can be created by specifying 'scratch' to the **status** argument of an **open()** function, with this syntax:

> **open(newunit=***unit-variable***, status='scratch', iostat=***io-variable***)**

As usual, the contents of a scratch file can be read by a program. When reading or writing file contents, the position within the file is dictated by the "file pointer". Fortran provides two functions that can be used to reposition the file pointer programmatically:

- **rewind()** – this function moves the file pointer to the beginning of the file, ready to read the first record.

- **backspace()** – this function moves the file pointer to just before the last record read.

Both of the above functions accept the file's unit number as their argument and can be used to modify the content of a scratch file.

scratch.f90

1 Begin a program that declares four variables
```
program main
    implicit none
    integer :: i, unit_num, ios
    integer, dimension(4) :: nums
```

2 Next, open a temporary scratch file and write data into it
```
open(newunit=unit_num, status='scratch', iostat=ios)
do i = 1, 4
    write(unit_num, *) i * 10
end do
```

3 Now, reposition the file pointer to the beginning of the temporary scratch file
```
rewind(unit_num)
```

4 Output the content of the scratch file
```
write(*, '(/,A)', advance='no') 'Initial data:'
do i = 1 ,4
    read(unit_num, *) nums(i)
    write(*, fmt='(I4)', advance='no') nums(i)
end do
```

5 Reposition the file pointer to the beginning of the scratch file again

```fortran
rewind(unit_num)
```

6 Read the first two records, then move the file pointer back to just before the second record

```fortran
read(unit_num, *) nums(1)
read(unit_num, *) nums(2)
backspace(unit_num)
```

7 Next, write data to update the scratch file's content

```fortran
write(unit_num, *) nums(2) + 5
write(unit_num, *) nums(3) * 2
write(unit_num, *) nums(4)
```

8 Reposition the file pointer to the beginning of the scratch file once more

```fortran
rewind(unit_num)
```

9 Output the updated content

```fortran
write(*, '(/,A)', advance='no') 'Updated data:'
do i = 1, 4
    read(unit_num, *) nums(i)
    write(*, fmt='(I4)', advance='no') nums(i)
end do
```

10 Finally, add a newline and close the scratch file

```fortran
print *
close(unit_num)
end program
```

11 Save the file named as **scratch.f90**, then compile and run the program to see the data read from a temporary file

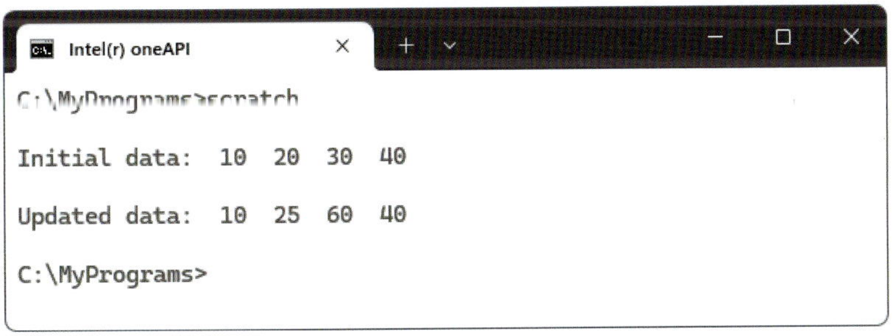

```
Intel(r) oneAPI              ×    +  ∨        —   □   ×

C:\MyPrograms>scratch

Initial data:  10  20  30  40

Updated data:  10  25  60  40

C:\MyPrograms>
```

Summary

- The declaration of a resizable character variable must include the **allocatable** keyword, and the **character** keyword should be followed by **(:)** to indicate that its length can be varied.

- User input can be imported into a program and be assigned to a variable by the **read()** function.

- The **write()** function allows a program to output to the screen or to a file.

- The **inquire()** function can be used to see if a file exists.

- A new file can be created by the **open()** function when its **status** argument specifies 'new'.

- The **unit** argument of the **open()** function must specify a unique unit number for the file.

- Fortran can automatically assign an unused unit number to a **newunit** argument, in place of the **unit** argument.

- After writing data into a file, the file should be closed by specifying its unit number as the argument to the **close()** function.

- Content can be appended to an existing file by the **open()** function when its **status** argument specifies 'old'.

- The **open()** function can include an **iostat** argument to capture the status of the input/output operation.

- If a file is opened without errors, the **iostat** status is **0**, otherwise it contains an error code.

- The **read()** function can be used to read data from a text file into a receiving variable.

- A temporary file can be created by the **open()** function when its **status** argument specifies 'scratch'.

- The **rewind()** function moves the file pointer to the beginning of the file, ready to read the first record.

- The **backspace()** function moves the file pointer to just before the last record read.

7 Storing procedures

This chapter demonstrates how to create reusable Fortran procedures as subroutines and functions.

Calling subroutines

The ability to create reusable blocks of code is a feature common to all modern programming languages. In Fortran these are called "procedures" and there are two types – functions and subroutines.

A subroutine is a reusable block of code that can be invoked whenever required to execute the statements within its code block. The subroutine code block begins with the **subroutine** keyword, followed by a chosen identifier name and **()** parentheses. The subroutine code block must be terminated by an **end subroutine** statement. In its most simple form, the syntax looks like this:

```
subroutine identifier-name()
    declarations
    statements-to-execute
end subroutine
```

In order to invoke a subroutine, to have it execute the statements it contains, the Fortran **call** keyword must be used in a statement that is followed by the subroutine's name and parentheses. For example, to invoke a subroutine named "greet":

```
call greet()
```

The subroutine can, optionally, accept arguments passed to it by the statement invoking the subroutine. The syntax of a subroutine code block then looks like this:

```
subroutine name( argument-name1, argument-name2, ... )
    declarations
    statements-to-execute
end subroutine
```

It is important to recognize that subroutines <u>can</u> modify the arguments passed to it. For example, to invoke a subroutine named "modify" that accepts two arguments:

```
call modify( x, y )
```

The subroutine in this case can manipulate the values of the arguments named **x** and **y** and is permitted to assign new values to like-named variables within its code block.

Subroutines <u>do not</u> return any value to the caller.

1 Begin a program that declares two variables

```fortran
program main
    implicit none
    integer(kind=1) :: a, b
```

sub.f90

2 Next, initialize the variables and output their values

```fortran
a = 4
b = 8
write(*, '(/,A)') 'Main Program...'
write(*, '(A,I2,4X,A,I2)' ) 'a =', a, 'b =', b
```

3 Now, call a "swap" subroutine, passing the variable values

```fortran
    call swap(a,b)
end program
```

4 Begin a subroutine that accepts two arguments and declares two like-named variables, plus one further variable

```fortran
subroutine swap(a,b)
    integer(kind=1) :: a, b, temp
```

5 Then, initialize the variables and output the values of the like-named variables

```fortran
    temp = a
    a = b
    b = temp
    write(*, '(/,A)' ) 'Subroutine...'
    write(*, '(A,I2,4X,A,I2)' ) 'a =', a, 'b =', b
end subroutine
```

A subroutine is able to modify its argument values and output the new values – but it does not return anything.

6 Save the program named as **sub.f90** then compile and run the program to see main program and subroutine output

```
Intel(r) oneAPI                    ×   +  ∨        —  □  ×

C:\MyPrograms>sub

Main Program...
a = 4     b = 8

Subroutine...
a = 8     b = 4

C:\MyPrograms>
```

Creating functions

In addition to the subroutine procedures described in the previous example, Fortran supports function procedures.

A function is a reusable block of code that can be invoked whenever required to execute the statements within its code block. The function code block begins with the **function** keyword, followed by a chosen identifier name and **()** parentheses. The function code block must be terminated by an **end function** statement. Its syntax looks like this:

```
function identifier-name(arg1, arg2, ...)
    declarations
    statements-to-execute
end function
```

In order to invoke a function, to have it execute the statements it contains, a statement simply requires the function's name and parentheses containing any arguments to be passed to the function. For example, to invoke a function named "compute":

```
compute( arg1, arg2 )
```

Unlike subroutine procedures that <u>do not</u> return anything, function procedures <u>do</u> return a single value. This value is known as the "function value".

To receive the returned function value, a variable of the appropriate data type must be declared in the structure containing the caller (e.g. the main program).

It is important to recognize that functions <u>cannot</u> modify the arguments passed to them.

Optionally, the function definition can, however, include a **result** keyword to specify the name of a variable in which to store the function's return value, with this syntax:

```
function identifier-name( arg1, arg2, ... ) result( variable-name )
    declarations
    statements-to-execute
end function
```

Adding a result variable can improve code readability and help avoid conflict with other variables.

1 Begin a program that declares three integer variables
```fortran
program main
    implicit none
    integer(kind=1) :: square, cube, num
```

func.f90

2 Next, add a loop that calls two functions on each iteration
```fortran
    do num = 2, 5
        write(*, '(/,I1,1X,A8,I3)' ) num, 'squared:', square(num)
        write(*,'(I1,1X,A6,I5)' ) num, 'cubed:', cube(num)
    end do
end program
```

3 Create a function that returns a value to the first variable
```fortran
function square( num )
    square = num**2
end function
```

4 Now, create another function that assigns a result and returns that value to the second variable
```fortran
function cube( num ) result( res )
    integer(kind=1) :: res
    res = num**3
end function
```

5 Save the program named as **func.f90**, then compile and run the program to see the returned function values

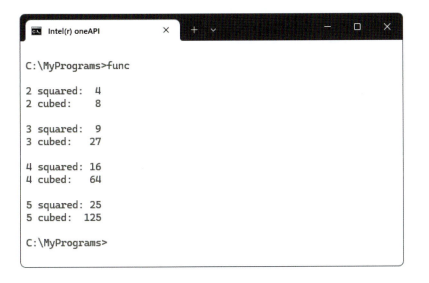

```
Intel(r) oneAPI                    ×   + ∨        —   □   ×

C:\MyPrograms>func

2 squared:   4
2 cubed:     8

3 squared:   9
3 cubed:    27

4 squared:  16
4 cubed:    64

5 squared:  25
5 cubed:   125

C:\MyPrograms>
```

Don't forget

A function is not able to modify its argument values – but it does return a function value.

111

Stating intent

In Fortran, limitations can be placed on how arguments passed to subroutines and functions can be used. To do this, placeholder "dummy argument" variables can first be associated with corresponding actual arguments to take on the actual argument value. Each dummy argument can then specify how the variable can be used by including an **intent** keyword within the dummy argument's declaration – with one of three possible values:

- **intent(in)** – this dummy argument is for input only, so it cannot be modified by the procedure. Its value can be used by the procedure to perform calculations but the value will not change during execution of the procedure. The value of the actual argument will be unchanged when the procedure ends:

```
subroutine double( num )
    integer, intent(in) :: num
    integer :: double
    double = num * 2
```

The actual argument value is used to calculate the value of another variable, but the actual argument remains unchanged.

- **intent(out)** – this dummy argument is for output only, so its value must be set by the procedure before it can be used for any calculations. Changes made to this dummy argument will be reflected in the actual argument when the procedure ends:

```
subroutine initialize( num )
    integer, intent(out) :: num
    num = 16
```

The argument value is undefined until set by the procedure.

- **intent(inout)** – this dummy argument is for both input and output. Its initial value is that of the actual argument but it can be modified during execution of the procedure. Changes made to this dummy argument will also be reflected in the actual argument when the procedure ends:

```
subroutine update( num )
    integer, intent( inout) :: num
    num = num * 2
```

The actual argument value will become double its initial value.

1 Begin a program that declares three integer variables
```fortran
program main
    implicit none
    integer(kind=1) :: a, b, c
```

intent.f90

2 Next, initialize the variables and output their values
```fortran
    a = 2
    b = 3
    c = 4
    write(*, '(/,A16,A6,I2,A6,I2,A6,I2)' ) &
        'Initial Values:', 'a =', a, 'b =', b, 'c =', c
```

3 Now, pass the variable values as arguments to a subroutine, then output their values once more
```fortran
    call compute(a,b,c)
    write(*, '(/,A16,A6,I2,A6,I3,A5,I3)' ) &
        'Final Values:', 'a =', a, 'b =', b, 'c =', c
end program
```

4 Now, begin a subroutine that associates dummy arguments with the actual argument values
```fortran
subroutine compute(a, b, c)
    integer(kind=1), intent(in) :: a
    integer(kind=1), intent(out) :: b
    integer(kind=1), intent(inout) :: c
```

5 Then, perform calculations using the dummy arguments
```fortran
    b = a * 10
    c = c * b
end subroutine
```

6 Save the program named as **intent.f90** then compile and run the program to see the returned variable values

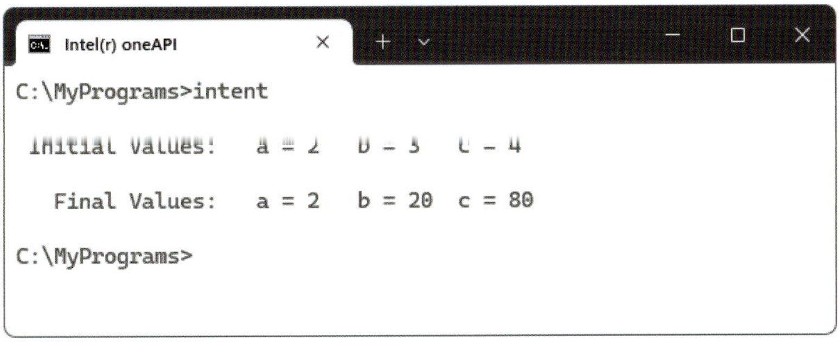

```
Intel(r) oneAPI                    ×    +  ⌄         —   □   ×

C:\MyPrograms>intent

 Initial Values:   a = 2   b = 3   c = 4

   Final Values:   a = 2   b = 20  c = 80

C:\MyPrograms>
```

Recurring calls

Subroutines and functions can call themselves "recursively" to emulate a loop structure. This requires the procedure declaration to begin with the **recursive** keyword.

As with loops it is important that recursive calls must modify a tested expression to avoid continuous execution – so the procedure will exit at some point.

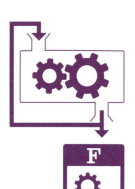

launch.f90

1 Create a program that calls a subroutine to make recursive calls until its argument value is decremented to zero

```fortran
program main
    implicit none
    call countdown(5)
end program
```

2 Next, begin a recursive subroutine that declares an integer dummy variable

```fortran
recursive subroutine countdown(num)
    integer(kind=1), intent(in) :: num
```

3 Now, add a conditional test to output the current variable value and decrement its value upon each recursive call

```fortran
if (num > 0 ) then
    write(*, '(6X,A,I4)' ) 'Countdown:', num
    call countdown(num-1)
else
    write(*, '(24X,A)' ) 'Lift Off!'
end if
end subroutine
```

4 Save the program named as **launch.f90** then compile and run the program to see the recursive variable values

```
Intel(r) oneAPI                    ×    +  ∨       —   □   ×

C:\MyPrograms>launch
        Countdown:    5
        Countdown:    4
        Countdown:    3
        Countdown:    2
        Countdown:    1
                        Lift Off!


C:\MyPrograms>
```

1 Begin a program that declares two variables and outputs a heading string

```fortran
program main
    implicit none
    integer(kind=1) :: step, fib
    write(*, '(/,A)' ) 'Fibonacci Sequence...'
```

recur.f90

2 Add a loop to call a recursive function 10 times

```fortran
    do step = 1, 10
        write(*,'(A5,I3,1X,A3,I5)' ) 'Step', step, 'is', fib(step)
    end do
end program
```

3 Next, begin a recursive function that declares an integer dummy variable and a regular integer variable

```fortran
recursive function fib(step) result(num)
    integer(kind=1), intent(in) :: step
    integer(kind=1) :: num
```

4 Now, add a conditional test that will return the calculated Fibonacci number upon each recursive call

```fortran
    if (step <= 1) then
        num = 1
    else
        num = fib(step-1) + fib(step-2)
    end if
end function
```

Hot tip

Fibonacci numbers are simply the sum of the previous two numbers in the sequence.

115

5 Save the program named as **recur.f90** then compile and run the program to see the recursive calculated values

```
Intel(r) oneAPI                               —  □  ×

C:\MyPrograms>recur

Fibonacci Sequence...
 Step  1  is     1
 Step  2  is     2
 Step  3  is     3
 Step  4  is     5
 Step  5  is     8
 Step  6  is    13
 Step  7  is    21
 Step  8  is    34
 Step  9  is    55
 Step 10  is    89

C:\MyPrograms>
```

Containing procedures

A Fortran program block can include internal procedures by heading a section with the **contains** keyword. The use of internal procedures can group related procedures for convenience. Most importantly, internal procedures can directly access the variables and data within the main program block. The syntax of a program block that includes internal procedures looks like this:

```
program program-name
    declarations
    statements-to-execute
contains
    internal-procedures
end program
```

Variables declared in the main program block are often referred to as "global" variables, as they are available globally to all internal procedures. The use of internal procedures usefully provides a degree of encapsulation, as their accessibility is limited to the containing program.

internal.f90

1 Begin a program that declares two integer variables, plus a character variable that will be initialized by an internal procedure call
```
program main
    implicit none
    integer(kind=1) :: a, b
    character(len=16) :: msg
```

2 First, initialize both integer variables
```
    a = 4
    b = 8
```

3 Next, add three statements to call internal subroutines
```
    call display(a,b)
    call swap(a,b)
    call display(a,b)
```

4 Now, output a string and call an internal function to obtain a calculated value for output
```
    write(*, '(/,A,I2)' ) 'Total:', add(a,b)
```

5 Then, output the character variable string value
```
    write(*, '(',A)' ) msg
```

6 Begin an internal procedure section within the program

```
contains
```

7 Create an internal subroutine procedure to simply output passed argument values

```
subroutine display(a,b)
    integer(kind=1), intent(in) :: a, b
    write(*,'(/,A,I2,4X,A,I2)' ) 'a=', a, 'b=', b
end subroutine
```

8 Create an internal subroutine procedure to manipulate the actual argument values in the main program

```
subroutine swap(a,b)
    integer(kind=1), intent(out) :: a, b
    integer(kind=1) :: temp
    temp = a
    a = b
    b = temp
end subroutine
```

9 Create an internal function to return a calculated value and to initialize the character variable in the program

```
function add(a,b) result(res)
    integer(kind=1), intent(in) :: a, b
    integer(kind=1) :: res
    res = a + b
    msg = 'Program Ends'
end function
end program
```

10 Save the program named as **internal.f90** then compile and run the program to see the internal procedures called

```
Intel(r) oneAPI                        ×    +  ∨      —  □  ×

C:\MyPrograms>internal

a= 4      b= 8

a= 8      b= 4

Total:12

Program Ends

C:\MyPrograms>
```

Using modules

Fortran code can be organized in "modules" that makes the code easier to manage, especially in larger programs. Modules can also be used by different programs so their procedures are reusable, and variables declared in modules are globally available to a program.

A module begins with the **module** keyword followed by an identifier name, and must be terminated by an **end module** statement. The body of a module consists of these two parts:

- **Specification Part** – an **implicit none** statement followed by declaration of variables, constants, and interfaces.

- **Contains Part** – a **contains** statement followed by function and subroutine definitions.

The syntax of a module therefore looks like this:

```
module identifier-name
    implicit none
        declarations
    contains
        procedure-definitions
end module
```

A Fortran program can incorporate a module, to make its features available to the program, by placing a **use** statement at the very start of its program block with this syntax:

```
use identifier-name
```

Multiple modules can be incorporated into a program by placing multiple **use** statements at the start of the program block.

Alternatively, an individual procedure can incorporate a module by placing a **use** statement at the very start of its procedure block.

If the program only requires access to one or more particular procedures, the **use** statement can be followed by an **only:** clause specifying the name/s of the required procedure/s:

```
use identifier-name only: procedure-name, procedure-name
```

The compilation of programs that use modules requires the ifx compiler to be given the program file name followed by the name of the module file/s.

Hot tip

It is good practice to include an **implicit none** statement both in the module code and program code.

...cont'd

1 Begin a module that contains a simple specification part
```fortran
module util
    implicit none
```

util.f90

2 Add a contains part that defines a function
```fortran
    contains

    function f_to_c(f) result(c)
        real :: f, c
        c = ( (f-32)*5) / 9    !°C = ( (°F-32)×5) / 9.
    end function
end module
```

3 Begin a program that incorporates the module above, and declares a real number variable
```fortran
program main
    use util, only:f_to_c
    implicit none
    real :: f
```

use.f90

4 Next, request user input to initialize the variable
```fortran
    write(*, '(/,A)', advance='no') &
        'Enter a Fahrenheit temperature: '
    read(*,*) f
```

5 Now, output a string that calls the function defined in the module to calculate a conversion
```fortran
    write(*, '(/,F4.1,1X,A)', advance='no') f, &
        'degrees Fahrenheit is'
    write(*,'(F5.1,1X,A)' ) f_to_c(f), 'degrees Celsius'
end program
```

6 Save the module as **util.f90** and the program as **use.f90** then compile and run the program to see the output

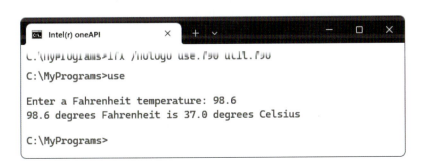

```
Intel(r) oneAPI         ×    +  ∨           —  □  ×

C:\MyPrograms>ifx /nologo use.f90 util.f90

C:\MyPrograms>use

Enter a Fahrenheit temperature: 98.6
98.6 degrees Fahrenheit is 37.0 degrees Celsius

C:\MyPrograms>
```

Beware

The compiled executable (**.exe**) file will have the same filename as the <u>first</u> file given to the compiler for compilation.

119

Restricting scope

Although variables and constants declared within a module have by default global scope, to be readily accessible by the program, their accessibility can be explicitly defined by including one of three possible access specifier keywords in their declaration:

- **public** – variables can be accessed from outside the module so that the program can read and modify their values, and constants can be read from outside the module.

- **protected** – variables and constants can be read from outside the module but the variable values cannot be modified.

- **private** – variables and constants cannot be accessed from outside the module, but both are accessible inside the module. These have only "local scope".

utils.f90

1 Begin a module containing a specification part that declares two variables plus a constant, which each include access specifiers

```
module utils
    implicit none
    real, public :: c
    real, protected :: freezing_point = 2**5
    real, parameter, private :: MULTIPLIER = 1.8
```

2 Next, add a **contains** part that defines a function

```
contains

    function f_to_c(f) result(c)
        real :: f, c
        c = ( (f-32)*5) / 9    ! °C = ( (°F-32)×5) / 9.
    end function
end module
```

3 Now, add a function that requires access to the non-global protected and private variables

```
    function c_to_f(c) result(f)
        real :: c, f
        f = (c * MULTIPLIER) + freezing_point   ! °F=°C*9/5+32
    end function

end module
```

4 Save the module named as **utils.f90**, ready for use by one or more programs

5   Begin a program that incorporates the module
```fortran
program main
    use utils
    implicit none
```

F

scope.f90

6   Next, request user input to initialize the public variable defined in the module
```fortran
write(*, '(/,A)', advance='no') &
    'Enter a Celsius temperature: '
read(*,*) c
```

7   Now, output a string that calls the function defined in the module to calculate a conversion
```fortran
write(*, '(/,F4.1,1X,A)', advance='no') c, &
    'degrees Celsius is'
write(*, '(1X,F4.1,1X,A)' ) c_to_f(c), 'degrees Fahrenheit'
```

8   Then, output the value of the protected variable defined in the module
```fortran
write(*,'(/,A,F4.1)' ) 'Fahrenheit freezing point:', &
    freezing_point
end program
```

9   Save the program as **scope.f90** then compile and run the program and module to see the output

```
Intel(r) oneAPI                  ×   +  ∨          —   □   ×

C:\MyPrograms>ifx /nologo scope.f90 utils.f90

C:\MyPrograms>scope

Enter a Celsius temperature: 37

37.0 degrees Celsius is 98.6 degrees Fahrenheit

Fahrenheit freezing point:32.0

C:\MyPrograms>
```

Summary

- A **subroutine** procedure is a reusable block of code that executes its statements when called, but returns nothing.

- The **call** keyword is required to invoke a **subroutine**.

- A **subroutine** can modify the arguments passed to it.

- A **function** procedure is a reusable block of code that executes its statements when called, and returns a single value.

- The **call** keyword is not required to invoke a **function**.

- A **function** cannot modify the arguments passed to it.

- A **function** definition can include a **result** keyword to specify the name of a variable in which to place its return value.

- Dummy argument variables are associated with corresponding actual arguments, and they take on the actual argument value.

- The declaration of a dummy argument can include an **intent** keyword to specify how the dummy argument may be used.

- The **intent** keyword may specify **in** for input only, or **out** for output only, or **inout** for both input and output.

- Changes made to a dummy argument are only reflected in the actual argument when the **intent** is **out** or **inout**.

- A **subroutine** or **function** can call itself recursively to emulate a loop structure when declared with the **recursive** keyword.

- A program block can include internal procedures by heading a section with the **contains** keyword.

- Internal procedures can directly access the variables and data within the main **program** block.

- A **module** has a specification part for declarations and a **contains** part for **function** and **subroutine** definitions.

- A program can incorporate a **module** by placing a **use** statement at the very start of its program block.

- The accessibility of module variables can be explicitly defined by the **public**, **protected**, and **private** access specifier keywords.

8 Using intrinsics

Numeric functions

Hot tip

The **aimag()** and **imag()** functions return the same result.

Function	Returns
abs(*n*)	the absolute value of *n*
aimag(*n*)	the imaginary part of complex *n*
aint(*n*)	real number *n* truncated toward zero
anint(*n*)	a real whole number nearest to *n*
ceiling(*n*)	the least integer greater than *n*
cmplx(*n1, n2*)	complex number of real numbers *n1*, *n2*
conjg(*n*)	the conjugate of complex number *n*
dble(*n*)	a double precision real number of *n*
dfloat(*n*)	a double precision real number from integer *n*
dim(*n1, n2*)	the positive difference between *n1*, *n2*
dot_product(*arr*)	the sum product of array elements
dprod(*n1, n2*)	the double precision product of *n1*, *n2*
floor(*n*)	the greatest integer less than *n*
ifix(*n*)	a truncated integer from single precision *n*
imag(*n*)	the imaginary part of complex *n*
int(*n*)	truncated real *n* as an integer
inum(*str*)	an integer (kind=2) of character string *str*
jnum(*str*)	an integer (kind=4) of character string *str*
knum(*str*)	an integer (kind=8) of character string *str*
matmul(*mx*)	the sum product of matrix elements
max(*n1, n2*)	the maximum value
min(*n1, n2*)	the minimum value
mod(*n1, n2*)	the remainder of *n1* divided by *n2*
nint(*n*)	the nearest integer to *n*
qcmplx(*n*)	quadruple precision complex of *n*
qfloat(*n*)	quadruple precision real of integer *n*
qnum(*str*)	quadruple precision real of character string *str*
qreal(*n*)	quadruple precision real part of complex *n*
real(*n*)	real number of integer *n*
rnum(*str*)	a real number of character string *str*
sign(*n1, n2*)	*n1* with the sign transferred from *n2*

1 Begin a program that declares three real constants, plus one character constant for formatting

```
program main
   implicit none
   real, parameter :: A = 25.75, B = 8.25, C = 5.5
   character(len=8), parameter :: LIST = '(A,F6.2)'
```

nums.f90

2 Next, display all real constant values

```
   print *
   write(*, LIST ) 'Constant a:', A
   write(*, LIST ) 'Constant b:', B
   write(*, LIST ) 'Constant c:', C
```

3 Now, output values returned by some numeric functions

```
   write(*, '(/,A,2X,A,I3)' ) 'Ceiling', 'a:', ceiling(A)
   write(*, '(A,4X,A,I3)' ) 'Floor', 'a:', floor(A)
   write(*, LIST ) 'Absolute a:', abs(A)
```

4 Then, output more values returned by numeric functions

```
   write(*, '(/,A,2X,A,F6.2)' ) 'Highest', 'a b c:', max(A,B,C)
   write(*, '(A,3X,A,F6.2)' ) 'Lowest', 'a b c:', min(A,B,C)
   write(*, LIST ) 'Difference a-b:', dim(A,B)
   write(*, '(A,2X,A,F6.2)' ) 'Remainder', 'a/b:', mod(A,B)
end program
```

5 Save the program as **nums.f90** then compile and run the program to see the returned results

```
C:\MyPrograms>nums

Constant a: 25.75
Constant b:  8.25
Constant c:  5.50

Ceiling  a: 26
Floor    a: 25
Absolute a: 25.75

Highest  a b c: 25.75
Lowest   a b c:  5.50
Difference a-b: 17.50
Remainder  a/b:  1.00

C:\MyPrograms>
```

125

Math functions

Function	Returns
acos(*n*)	the arccosine of *n* in radians
acosd(*n*)	the arccosine of *n* in degrees
acosh(*n*)	the hyperbolic arccosine of *n*
asin(*n*)	the arcsine of *n* in radians
asind(*n*)	the arcsine of *n* in degrees
asinh(*n*)	the hyperbolic arcsine of *n*
atan(*n*)	the arctangent of *n* in radians
atand(*n*)	the arctangent of *n* in degrees
atanh(*n*)	the hyperbolic arctangent of *n*
bessel_j0(*n*)	the Bessel function result, first kind, order 0
bessel_j1(*n*)	the Bessel function result, first kind, order 1
bessel_jn(*n1, n2*)	the Bessel function result, first kind, order *n1*
bessel_y0(*n*)	the Bessel function result, second kind, order 0
bessel_y1(*n*)	the Bessel function result, second kind, order 1
bessel_yn(*n1, n2*)	the Bessel function result, second kind, order *n1*
cos(*n*)	the cosine of *n* in radians
cosd(*n*)	the cosine of *n* in degrees
cosh(*n*)	the hyperbolic cosine of *n*
cotan(*n*)	the cotangent on *n* in radians
cotand(*n*)	the cotangent on *n* in degrees
exp(*n*)	the exponential value of *n*
exp10(*n*)	the base 10 exponential value of *n*
gamma(*n*)	the gamma value of *n*
hypot(*n1, n2*)	the length of the hypotenuse for sides *n1, n2*
log(*n*)	the natural logarithm of *n*
log10(*n*)	the common logarithm of *n*
sin(*n*)	the sine of *n* in radians
sind(*n*)	the sine of *n* in degrees
sinh(*n*)	the hyperbolic sine of *n*
sqrt(*n*)	the square root of *n*
tan(*n*)	the tangent of *n* in radians
tand(*n*)	the tangent of *n* in degrees
tanh(*n*)	the hyperbolic tangent of *n*

Hot tip

Radians are units of measurement for angles. Degrees can be converted to radians using the formula **degrees x π/180**. For example, **90** degrees x **π / 180 = 1.5708** radians. Similarly, radians can be converted to degrees with **radians x 180/π**. For example, **1.5708** radians x 180 / **π = 90** degrees.

...cont'd

1 Begin a program that declares three real constants, plus one character constant for formatting

```
program main
    implicit none
    real, parameter :: A = 64.0, B = 32.0, C = 16.0
    character(len=8), parameter :: LIST = '(A,F6.2)'
```

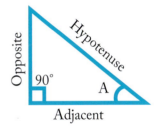

math.f90

2 Next, display all real constant values

```
    print *
    write(*, LIST ) 'Constant a:', A
    write(*, LIST ) 'Constant b:', B
    write(*, LIST ) 'Constant c:', C
```

3 Output trigonometric values returned by math functions

```
    write(*, '(/,A,F6.2,A8)' ) 'Sine of b:   ', sind(B), 'degrees'
    write(*, '(A,F6.2,A8)' ) 'Cosine of b: ', cosd(B), 'degrees'
    write(*, (A,F6.2,A8)' ) 'Tangent of b:', tand(B), 'degrees'
```

4 Then, output more values returned by math functions

```
    print *
    write(*, LIST ) 'Square Root of a:', sqrt(A)
    write(*, LIST ) 'Log(base10) of c:', log10(C)
    write(*, LIST ) 'Hypotenuse - 3,4:', hypot(3,4)
end program
```

5 Save the program as **math.f90** then compile and run the program to see the returned results

```
C:\MyPrograms>math

Constant a: 64.00
Constant b: 32.00
Constant c: 16.00

Sine of b:    0.53 degrees
Cosine of b:  0.85 degrees
Tangent of b: 0.62 degrees

Square Root of a:  8.00
Log(base10) of c:  1.20
Hypotenuse - 3,4:  5.00

C:\MyPrograms>
```

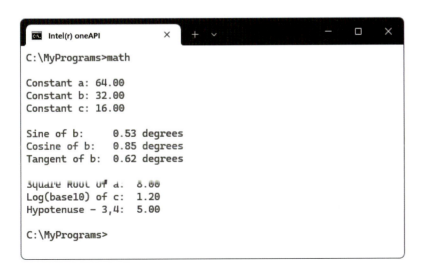

$$sine\ A = \frac{opposite}{hypotenuse}$$

$$cosine\ A = \frac{adjacent}{hypotenuse}$$

$$tangent\ A = \frac{opposite}{adjacent}$$

Inquiry functions

Function	Returns
associated(*ptr*)	a true or false Boolean value describing whether pointer *ptr* has an associated target
baddress(*n*)	the memory address of argument *n*
digits(*n*)	the number of binary digits in *n*
eof(*f*)	a true or false Boolean value describing whether the end of file *f* has been reached or exceeded
epsilon(*n*)	the smallest positive number of the same kind as *n*
huge(*n*)	the largest possible number for numbers of the same kind as *n*
isnan(*n*)	a true or false Boolean value describing whether floating point *n* is not a number
loc(*n*)	the memory address of *n*
logical(*expr*)	the logical value of expression *expr* or of a logical variable
maxexponent(*n*)	the maximum exponent for numbers of the same kind as *n*
minexponent(*n*)	the minimum exponent for numbers of the same kind as *n*
new_line()	a newline character
out_of_range(*n1,n2*)	a true or false Boolean value describing whether *n2* is beyond the range *n1*
precision(*n*)	the precision of floating point number *n*
present(*n*)	a true or false Boolean value describing whether optional dummy argument *n* has an associated actual argument
radix(*n*)	an integer representing the base numbering system used to represent *n*
range(*n*)	the decimal exponent range for numbers of the same kind as *n*
tiny(*n*)	the smallest possible number for numbers of the same kind as floating point number *n*

Hot tip

Typically, the radix for both **integer** and **real** numbers is 2 – indicating the binary numbering system.

...cont'd

① Begin a program that declares two constants

```
program main
    implicit none
    integer(kind=1), dimension(3), parameter :: ARR = [7,9,13]
    real(kind=4), parameter :: NUM = 13.0
```

inqs.f90

② Next, output the array values and its memory address

```
    write(*, '(/,A,3I5)' ) 'Array:', ARR
    write(*, '(A12,Z12,/)' ) 'Array at: 0x', loc(ARR)
```

③ Now, output the array element memory addresses

```
    write(*, '(A13,Z12)' ) 'Element 1: 0x', baddress( ARR(1) )
    write(*, '(A13,Z12)' ) 'Element 2: 0x', baddress( ARR(2) )
    write(*, '(A13,Z12)' ) 'Element 3: 0x', baddress( ARR(3) )
```

④ Then, confirm that the floating point value is indeed a number, and output some of the properties for its kind

```
    write(*, '(/,F4.1,A17,L2)' ) NUM, &
        'Is Not A Number:', isnan(NUM)
    write(*, '(/,A,I11)' ) 'Maximum possible:', huge(NUM)
    write(*, '(A,F5.2)' ) 'Minimum possible:', tiny(NUM)
    write(*, '(A,I4)' ) 'Maximum exponent:', &
        maxexponent(NUM)
end program
```

⑤ Save the program as **inqs.f90** then compile and run the program to see the returned results

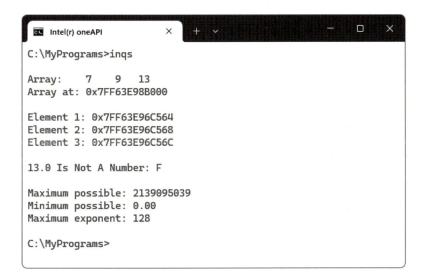

```
C:\MyPrograms>inqs

Array:    7    9   13
Array at: 0x7FF63E98B000

Element 1: 0x7FF63E96C564
Element 2: 0x7FF63E96C568
Element 3: 0x7FF63E96C56C

13.0 Is Not A Number: F

Maximum possible: 2139095039
Minimum possible: 0.00
Maximum exponent: 128

C:\MyPrograms>
```

Character functions

Function	Returns
achar(_n_)	the character at ASCII character code _n_
adjustl(_str_)	the string _str_ left-aligned in allocated space by moving any leading space to trailing space
adjustr(_str_)	the string _str_ right-aligned in allocated space by moving any trailing space to leading space
char(_n_)	the _n_th character in the system processor's character set
iachar(_c_)	the position of character _c_ in the ASCII character code
ichar(_c_)	the position of character _c_ in the system processor's character set
index(_str, sub_)	the starting position of substring _sub_ within string _str_
len(_str_)	the allocated length of string _str_
len_trim(_str_)	the length of string _str_ without trailing spaces
lge(_str1, str2_)	a true or false Boolean value describing whether string _str1_ is lexically greater than or equal to string _str2_
lgt(_str1, str2_)	a true or false Boolean value describing whether _str1_ is lexically greater than _str2_
lle(_str1, str2_)	a true or false Boolean value describing whether string _str1_ is lexically less than or equal to string _str2_
lgt(_str1, str2_)	a true or false Boolean value describing whether _str1_ is lexically less than _str2_
repeat(_str, n_)	the string _str_ repeated _n_ times
scan(_str1, str2_)	the position in string _str1_ of the first case-sensitive character found in string set _str2_
trim(_str_)	the string _str_ with trailing spaces removed
verify(_str1, str2_)	the position of the first case-sensitive character in string _str1_ that is absent in string _str2_, or 0 if all characters in _str2_ do appear in _str1_

Hot tip

Lexical comparison in Fortran is based on the ASCII character code values. For example, 'A' (65) is less than 'Z' (90).

...cont'd

1 Begin a program that declares a character string variable plus an integer counter variable

```fortran
program main
    implicit none
    character(:), allocatable :: str
    integer(kind=1) :: i
```

char.f90

2 Next, allocate string space and output the allocated length

```fortran
    allocate(character(32) :: str)
    write(*,'(/,A,I2)' ) 'Allocated space:', len(str)
```

3 Now, initialize the string and output its occupied length

```fortran
    str = 'Keep calm and carry on.'
    write(*,'(2A)' ) 'String assigned:', str
    write(*,'(A,I2,/)' ) 'Space occupied:', len(str)
```

4 Then, add a loop to output the alphabet in uppercase

```fortran
    write(*,'(A)', advance='no') 'Uppercase alphabet:'
    do i = 65, 90
        write(*,'(A1)', advance='no') achar(i)
    end do
```

5 Finally, output the ASCII code of a letter, and the letter at a specified ASCII code value

```fortran
    write(*,'(/,A,I2)' ) 'Character Code of A:', iachar('A')
    write(*,'(2A)' ) 'Letter at ASCII Code 97:', char(97)
    deallocate(str)
end program
```

6 Save the program as **char.f90** then compile and run the program to see the returned results

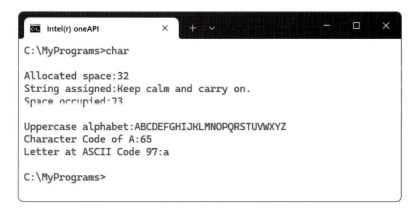

```
C:\MyPrograms>char

Allocated space:32
String assigned:Keep calm and carry on.
Space occupied:23

Uppercase alphabet:ABCDEFGHIJKLMNOPQRSTUVWXYZ
Character Code of A:65
Letter at ASCII Code 97:a

C:\MyPrograms>
```

Float functions

Function	Returns
exponent(*n*)	the exponent part of the model representation of floating point number *n*
fraction(*n*)	the fractional part of the model representation of floating point number *n*
nearest(*n, s*)	the nearest different processor number to floating point number *n* in the direction of infinity with the same sign as sign *s*
rrspacing(*n*)	the reciprocal of the relative spacing of model numbers near number *n*
scale(*n, i*)	the value of the exponent part of floating point number *n* changed by integer *i*
set_exponent(*n, i*)	the value of the exponent part of floating point number *n* set to integer *i*
spacing(*n*)	the absolute spacing of model numbers near floating point number *n*

Kind functions

Function	Returns
kind(*n*)	the kind parameter value of number *n*
selected_int_kind(*p*)	the kind of integer required for precision *p* number of digits
selected_real_kind(*p*)	the kind of real required for precision *p* number of digits

Logical function

Function	Returns
logical(*bool*)	the current Boolean true or false value of logical *bool*

...cont'd

kind.f90

1 Begin a program that declares four variables

```fortran
program main
    implicit none
    real(kind=4) :: num, frac_part
    integer(kind=4) :: expo_part
    logical :: flag
```

2 Next, initialize all four variables

```fortran
num = 18.50
flag = .true.
expo_part = exponent(num)
frac_part = num / 10.0**expo_part
```

3 Now, output three variable values

```fortran
write(*, '(/,A,F9.2)' ) 'Number:', num
write(*, '(A,ES)' ) 'Mantissa:', frac_part
write(*, '(A,I3)' ) 'Exponent:', expo_part
```

4 Then, output required kinds for specified precisions

```fortran
write(*, '(/,A,I4)' ) 'Kind of real for 12 digits:', &
    selected_real_kind(12)
write(*, '(A,I2)' ) 'Kind of integer for 3 digits:', &
    selected_int_kind(3)
```

The edit descriptor **ES** is used here to format the calculated mantissa in scientific notation.

5 Finally, output the logical value and kind

```fortran
write(*, '(/,A,L)' ) 'Logical:', logical(flag)
write(*, '(A,I2)' ), 'Logical default kind:', kind(flag)
```

6 Save the program as **kind.f90** then compile and run the program to see the returned results

```
Intel(r) oneAPI                    ×    + ∨       —   □   ×

C:\MyPrograms>kind

Number:    18.50
Mantissa:  1.8500000E-04
Exponent:  5

Kind of real for 12 digits:    8
Kind of integer for 3 digits: 2

Logical: T
Logical default kind: 4

C:\MyPrograms>
```

Bit functions

Function	Returns
ble(*n1, n2*)	true if *n1* is bitwise less than or equal to *n2*
bit(*n1, n2*)	true if *n1* is bitwise less than *n2*
btest(*n, pos*)	true if bit at position *pos* in number *n* is set (1)
dshiftl(*n1, n2, n*)	combined *n1* and *n2* shifted left by *n* places
dshiftr(*n1, n2, n*)	combined *n1* and *n2* shifted right by *n* places
iand(*n1, n2*)	result of bitwise **AND** on integers *n1* and *n2*
ibchng(*n, pos*)	reverse of bit in integer *n* at position *pos*
ibclr(*n, pos*)	cleared to zero bit in integer *n* at position *pos*
ibits(*n, pos, len*)	bits in integer *n* from position *pos* for length *len*
ibset(*n, pos*)	bit in integer *n* at position *pos* set (1)
ieor(*n1, n2*)	result of bitwise **XOR** on integers *n1* and *n2*
ior(*n1, n2*)	result of bitwise **OR** on integers *n1* and *n2*
isha(*n1, n*)	arithmetic shift of number *n1* bits by *n* places
ishc(*n1, n*)	circular shift of number *n1* bits by *n* places
ishft(*n1, n*)	left shift of number *n1* bits by *n* places
ishftc(*n1, n, len*)	circular shift of *n1* bits of length *len* by *n* places
ishl(*n1, n*)	end-off shift left of number *n1* bits by *n* places
lshift(*n1, n*)	left shift of number *n1* bits by *n* places
maskl(*n*)	left-justified mask of number *n*
maskr(*n*)	right-justified mask of number *n*
merge_bits(*n1, n2, mask*)	combined bits of numbers *n1* and *n2* according to bit values in number *mask*
not(*n*)	the reverse of all bit values in number *n*
or(*n1, n2*)	the result of bitwise **OR** on integers *n1* and *n2*
rshift(*n1, n*)	right shift of number *n1* bits by *n* places
shifta(*n1, n*)	arithmetic shift of number *n1* bits by *n* places
shiftl(*n1, n*)	left shift of number *n1* bits by *n* places
shiftr(*n1, n*)	right shift of number *n1* bits by *n* places
xor(*n1, n*)	the result of bitwise **XOR** on integers *n1* and *n2*

1 Begin a program that declares three integer variables

```
program main
    implicit none
    integer(kind=2) :: n1, n2, n
```

F

bits.f90

2 Next, initialize two variables and output their decimal and binary values

```
n1 = 213
n2 = 120
write(*, '(/,A,I14,B12.8)' ) 'Number 1:', n1, n1
write(*, '(A,I14,B12.8)' ) 'Number 2:', n2, n2
```

3 Now, output the Least Significant Bit values

```
write(*, '(/,A,L10)' ), 'LSB Set (1):', btest(n1, 0)
write(*, '(A,L10)' ), 'LSB Set (2):', btest(n2, 0)
n = ibchng(n1, 0)
write(*, '(A,I8,B12.8)' ) 'LSB Change (1):', n, n
n = ibset(n1, 0)
write(*, '(A,I9,B12.8)' ) 'LSB Reset (1):', n, n
```

4 Then, output manipulated bit values

```
n = ibclr(n1, 2)
write(*, '(/,A18,I5,B12.8)' ) 'Bit 2 Clear (1):', n, n
n = isha(n2, -1)
write(*, '(A18,I5,B12.8)' ) 'Shift Right (2):', n, n
n = merge_bits(n1, n2, n1 )
write(*, '(A18,I5,B12.8)' ) 'Merged Bits (1&2):', n, n
```

5 Save the program as **bits.f90** then compile and run the program to see the returned results

```
 Intel(r) oneAPI            ×    +  ˅           —   □   ×

C:\MyPrograms>bits

Number 1:           213      11010101
Number 2:           120      01111000

LSB Set (1):          T
LSB Set (2):          F
LSB Change (1):     212      11010100
LSB Reset (1):      213      11010101

  Bit 2 Clear (1):  209      11010001
  Shift Right (2):   60      00111100
Merged Bits (1&2):  253      11111101

C:\MyPrograms>
```

Array functions

Function	Returns
all(*arr*)	true if all elements in array *arr* are true
allocated(*arr*)	true if memory is allocated for array *arr*
any(*arr*)	true if any element in array *arr* is true
cshift(*arr, n*)	array *arr* elements circular shifted *n* places
count(*arr*)	the number of true elements in array *arr*
eoshift(*arr, n*)	array *arr* elements end-off shifted *n* places
findloc(*arr, val*)	the position of value *val* within array *arr*
iall(*arr*)	an integer after bitwise **AND** reduction of *arr*
iany(*arr*)	an integer after bitwise **OR** reduction of *arr*
is_contiguous(*arr*)	true if elements in array *arr* are contiguous
iparity(*arr*)	an integer after bitwise **XOR** reduction of *arr*
lbound(*arr*)	an integer that is the lower bound of array *arr*
maxloc(*arr*)	the index position of the largest value in *arr*
maxval(*arr*)	the largest value in array *arr*
merge(*arr1, arr2, mask*)	element values from arrays *arr1* and *arr2* according to logical array *mask* values
minloc(*arr*)	the index position of the largest value in *arr*
minval(*arr*)	the smallest value in array *arr*
norm2(*arr*)	the square root of the sum of the squares of the element values in array *arr*
pack(*arr, mask*)	elements in array *arr* that are true in *mask*
parity(*mask*)	a Boolean after bitwise **XOR** reduction of *mask*
product(*arr*)	the sum of multiplying all elements in array *arr*
rank(*arr*)	the number of dimensions in array *arr*
reshape(*arr, sh*)	array *arr* with different shape *sh*
shape(*arr*)	the shape of array *arr*
size(*arr*)	the total number of elements in array *arr*
spread(*arr*)	replicated array *arr* with an added dimension
sum(*arr*)	the total of all element values in array *arr*
transpose(*arr*)	array *arr* with rows and columns swapped
ubound(*arr*)	an integer that is the upper bound of array *arr*
unpack(*arr2, mask, arr1*)	an array of *arr1* element values where true in *mask* or *arr2* element values where false

...cont'd

1 Begin a program that declares three arrays
```fortran
program main
    implicit none
    integer(kind=2), dimension(5) :: arr1, arr2
    logical, dimension(5) :: mask
```

arrs.f90

2 Next, initialize all three arrays
```fortran
arr1 = [1,2,3,4,5]
arr2 = [10,20,30,40,50]
mask = [0,-1,0,-1,0]
write(*, '(/,A,5I3,/,A,5I3,/,A,5L3,/)' ), &
    '1:',arr1, '2:', arr2, '3:', mask
```

3 Now, output some array values
```fortran
write(*, '(A,5I4)' ), 'Product (1):', product(arr1)
write(*, '(A,5I4)' ), 'Maximum (2):', maxval(arr2)
write(*, '(A,5I4)' ), 'Sum (1 & 2):', sum(arr1)+sum(arr2)
```

The Least Significant Bit (LSB) is the right-most bit and is at position 0. This means that the bit at position 2 is third from the right.

137

4 Then, output manipulated array elements
```fortran
write(*, '(/,A16,5I3)' ), 'Packed:', pack(arr1, mask)
write(*, '(A16,5I3)' ), 'End-off Shift:', eoshift(arr1, 2)
write(*, '(A16,5I3)' ), 'Unpacked:', &
    unpack(arr2, mask, arr1)
write(*, '(A16,5I3)' ), 'Merged:', merge(arr1, arr2, mask)
end program
```

5 Save the program as **arrs.f90** then compile and run the program to see the returned results

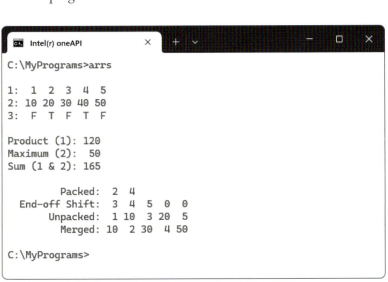

```
Intel(r) oneAPI              ×    +  ⌄         —   ☐   ×

C:\MyPrograms>arrs

1:  1  2  3  4  5
2: 10 20 30 40 50
3:  F  T  F  T  F

Product (1): 120
Maximum (2):  50
Sum (1 & 2): 165

        Packed:  2  4
 End-off Shift:  3  4  5  0  0
      Unpacked:  1 10  3 20  5
        Merged: 10  2 30  4 50

C:\MyPrograms>
```

Reading right-to-left, the bits represent values of 1, 2, 4, 8, 16, 32, 64, etc.

Reduce function

Fortran provides a special **reduce()** function that allows an array to be reduced to a single value by a specified custom function. The **reduce()** function requires two arguments to specify the array name and the custom function name. The function must be declared with the **pure** keyword – denoting it will have no side effects – and must have two arguments with associated dummy arguments defined with **intent(in)** attributes.

reduce.f90

1 Begin a program that declares an array constant

```
program main
    implicit none
    integer, dimension(5), parameter :: ARR = [1, 2, 3, 4, 5]
```

2 Next, add statements to output the array element values and the result of two reductions

```
    write(*, '(/,A16,5I3)' ) 'Array:', ARR
    write(*, '(A16,I5)' ) 'Sum:', reduce(ARR, sum_op)
    write(*, '(A16,I5)' ) 'Product:', reduce(ARR, mul_op)
```

3 Now, add a **contains** section with two custom functions

```
    contains
        pure function sum_op(a, b) result(res)
            integer, intent(in) :: a, b
            integer :: res
            res = a + b
        end function

        pure function mul_op(a, b) result(res)
            integer, intent(in) :: a, b
            integer :: res
            res = a * b
        end function
end program
```

4 Save the file as **reduce.f90** then compile and run the program to see the results output from custom functions

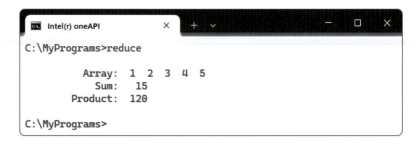

9 Programming objects

Encapsulating data

Real world objects have properties and behaviors that can be represented in Object Oriented Programming (OOP) in Fortran. Variables can store the object properties, and procedures can emulate the object behaviors. For example, a car has properties of body color and style, plus behaviors of acceleration and braking.

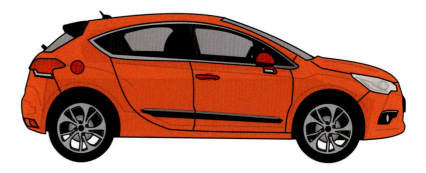

The variables and procedures representing an object are contained within a Fortran "class". These are collectively known as its "members", and the procedures are known as its "methods".

Access to class members from outside the class is controlled by access specifiers in the class declaration. Typically, **private** will deny access to the variables but allow access to "setter" and "getter" methods that can store and retrieve data from the variables. This technique of data hiding ensures that stored data is safely encapsulated within the class variable members, and is the first principle of OOP.

A class is first defined within a **module** using the **type** keyword followed by a name of choice for the class – adhering to the usual Fortran naming conventions but beginning in uppercase. Next come the access specifier followed by class member declarations. The getter and setter procedure names are listed within a **contains** section after a **procedure** keyword. The syntax looks like this:

```
type Class-name
    access-specifier
        variable-declarations
    contains
        procedure :: subroutine-name, function-name, ...
end type
```

Having defined a derived base **type** at the beginning of a **module** a **contains** section can be added to the module in which to define the getter and setter methods declared in the base type definition.

The setter and getter procedure definitions must receive a reference to the base type by including a **this** identifier as an argument. Then, a dummy argument can be associated to the actual argument referencing the base type definition. This dummy argument declaration begins with a **class** keyword followed by parentheses specifying the name given to the base type. The declaration should also include an **intent** attribute to specify how the dummy argument can be used. The **this** identifier is then specified to reference the current instance of the base type. The syntax of a setter method begins like this:

```
subroutine procedure-name ( this )
   class( type-name ), intent(out) :: this
```

Members of a class are addressed by stating the class name followed by the **%** symbol and the member name – for example, to address a **color** variable member of a **Car** class with **Car%color**.

When a variable class member is not absolutely required to be initialized by a setter method, its declaration can include the **optional** keyword. Usefully, a default value for an optional variable can be specified after testing whether it has been omitted by stating its name as the argument to an intrinsic **present()** function. For example, for an optional **color** variable:

```
if ( present( color ) ) then
   this%color = color
else
   this%color = 'red'
end if
```

A class can be used in a program by making the module available with a **use** statement stating the module name as usual. Instances of the class can then be created by a **type()** statement, like this:

```
type( Class-name ) :: instance-name, instance-name, ...
```

The getter and setter class methods are addressed by stating the instance name followed by the **%** symbol and the method name – for example, to address a **set_color**() setter method of a **Fiesta** instance of a **Car** class with **call Fiesta%set_color(color-name)**.

Creating classes

dog.f90

1 Begin a module that defines a class type, which declares two private variables and three private procedures

```
module class_Dog
   implicit none

   type Dog
      private
         integer(kind=1)  :: age
         character(len=5) :: fur
      contains
         procedure :: set_dog, get_age, get_fur
   end type
```

2 Next, begin a module **contains** section

```
   contains
```

3 Now, begin a subroutine that accepts three arguments and declares dummy variables for each argument

```
      subroutine set_dog(this, age, fur)
         class(Dog), intent(out) :: this
         integer, intent(in) :: age
         character(len=5), intent(in), optional :: fur
```

Hot tip

Notice that a default value will be assigned if no value is specified for the optional variable by the caller.

4 Then, add statements to assign values to the class variables

```
         this%age = age
         if ( present(fur) ) then
            this%fur = fur
         else
            this%fur = 'black'
         end if
      end subroutine
```

5 Add functions to return values stored in the class variables when called, then save the file as **dog.f90**

```
      function get_age(this) result(age)
         class(Dog), intent(in) :: this
         integer :: age
         age = this%age
      end function

      function get_fur(this) result(fur)
         class(Dog), intent(in) :: this
         character(len=5) :: fur
         fur = this%fur
      end function
   end module
```

...cont'd

1 Begin a program that will use the **Dog** class created on the opposite page

```
program main
    use class_Dog
    implicit none
```

2 Next, create two instances of the **Dog** class

```
type(Dog) :: Fido, Coco
```

3 Now, call the **Dog** class setter subroutine to initialize class member variables, specifying a value for each one

```
call Fido%set_dog(3, 'brown')
```

4 Then, call the **Dog** class setter subroutine to initialize class member variables, omitting an optional variable value

```
call Coco%set_dog(5)
```

5 Finally, call the **Dog** class getter functions to output the stored class member variable value for each instance

```
write(*, '(/,A10,I2,A10,A6,A7)' ) 'Fido is a', &
    Fido%get_age(),'month old', Fido%get_fur(), 'puppy.'

write(*,'(/,A10,I2,A10,A6,A7)' ) 'Coco is a', &
    Coco%get_ age(),'month old', Coco%get_fur(), 'puppy.'
end program
```

6 Save the file as **encap.f90** then compile and run the program and module to see the output

encap.f90

Don't forget

The **use** statement must appear at the beginning of the program code block.

143

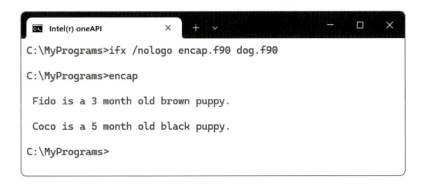

```
C:\MyPrograms>ifx /nologo encap.f90 dog.f90

C:\MyPrograms>encap

 Fido is a 3 month old brown puppy.

 Coco is a 5 month old black puppy.

C:\MyPrograms>
```

Inheriting properties

A Fortran class can be created as a brand new class, like that in the previous example, or can be derived from an existing class. Importantly, a derived class inherits members of the parent (base) class from which it is derived – in addition to its own members. The ability to inherit members from a base class allows derived classes to be created that share certain common properties, which have been defined in the base class. For example, a "Polygon" base class may define width and height properties that are common to all polygons. Classes of "Rectangle" and Triangle" could be derived from the Polygon class – inheriting width and height properties, in addition to their own members defining their unique features.

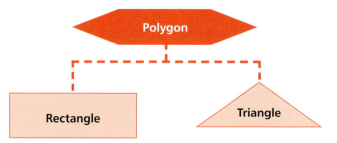

The virtue of inheritance is extremely powerful and is the second principle of OOP. A derived class **type** definition includes an **extends** keyword in the specification, followed by parentheses stating the base class name.

shape.f90

1 Begin a module that defines a base class type and defines two derived classes

```
module class_Shape
   implicit none
   type Polygon
     private
        integer(kind=4) :: width, height
   contains
        procedure :: set_values
   end type

   type, extends(Polygon) :: Rectangle
   contains
      procedure :: rectangle_area
   end type

   type, extends(Polygon) :: Triangle
   contains
      procedure :: triangle_area
   end type
```

2 Next, add a **contains** section with setter and getter methods, then save the file as **shape.f90**

```
contains
subroutine set_values(this, width, height)
    class(Polygon), intent(out) :: this
    integer(kind=4), intent(in) :: width, height
    this%width = width
    this%height = height
end subroutine

function rectangle_area(this) result(area)
    class(Rectangle), intent(in) :: this
    integer(kind=4) :: area
    area = this%width * this%height
end function

function triangle_area(this) result(area)
    class(Triangle), intent(in) :: this
    integer(kind=4) :: area
    area = (this%width * this%height) / 2
end function
end module
```

3 Produce a program that creates instances of the derived classes, initializes their variables, then outputs their values

```
program main
    use class_Shape
    implicit none
    type( Rectangle ) :: quad
    type( Triangle ) :: triad
    call quad%set_values(4,5)
    call triad%set_values(4,5)
    write(*, '(/,A,I5)' ) 'Rectangle Area:', quad%rectangle_area()
    write(*, '(A,I5)' )  'Triangle Area: ', triad%triangle_area()
end program
```

inherit.f90

4 Save the file as **inherit.f90** then compile and run the program and module to see the output

```
C:\MyPrograms>inherit

Rectangle Area:    20
Triangle Area:    10

C:\MyPrograms>
```

Redirecting methods

Methods defined in a base class type and derived class type can be redirected using the `=>` pointer association operator. This directs the same method name defined in both to procedures with different names. Calling a class method will then invoke the method associated with a particular instance.

length.f90

1 Begin a module that defines a base class type with a method associated with another method name

```
module class_Length
   implicit none
   type :: Length
      private
      real(kind=4) :: x
      contains
      procedure :: get_length, set => set_yards
   end type
```

2 Next, define a derived class with a method associated by another different name

```
   type, extends(Length) :: Metric
      private
      contains
      procedure :: set => set_meters
   end type
```

3 Now, add associated setter methods and a getter method, then save the file as **length.f90**

```
   contains
      subroutine set_yards(this, n)
         class(Length), intent(out) :: this
         real(kind=4), intent(in) :: n
         this%x = n * 0.3333
      end subroutine

      subroutine set_meters(this, n)
         class(Metric), intent(out) :: this
         real(kind=4), intent(in) :: n
         this%x = n * 0.3048
      end subroutine

      function get_length(this) result(length)
         class(Length), intent(in) :: this
         real(kind=4) :: length
         length = this%x
      end function
end module
```

4 Begin a program that declares a variable and creates instances of the base class and the derived class

```fortran
program main
    use class_Length
    implicit none
    real(kind=4) :: feet
    type(Length) :: yards
    type(Metric) :: meters
```

override.f90

5 Next, add statements requesting user input to initialize the program variable

```fortran
write(*, '(/,A)', advance='no') 'Enter a Distance in Feet: '
read(*,*) feet
```

6 Now, add statements to initialize the class instance variables by calling the same method name

```fortran
call yards%set(feet)
call meters%set(feet)
```

7 Then, add statements to output the value of the relative instance variables

```fortran
write(*, '(/,A8,F6.3)' ) 'Yards:', yards%get_length()
write(*, '(A8,F6.3)' ) 'Meters:', meters%get_length()
end program
```

8 Save the file as **override.f90** then compile and run the program and module to see the output

```
Intel(r) oneAPI                    ×   + ∨              —   □   ×

C:\MyPrograms>ifx /nologo override.f90 length.f90

C:\MyPrograms>override

Enter a Distance in Feet: 3

  Yards: 1.000
 Meters: 0.914

C:\MyPrograms>override

Enter a Distance in Feet: 3.28

  Yards: 1.093
 Meters: 1.000

C:\MyPrograms>
```

Enabling polymorphism

The three cornerstones of OOP are encapsulation, inheritance, and polymorphism. The term "polymorphism" (from Greek, meaning "many forms") describes the ability to assign a different meaning, or purpose, to an entity according to its context. The previous example achieves a degree of polymorphism by associating different procedures with one name.

In Fortran, polymorphism can also be achieved by "overloading" procedures, in which the same procedure name can be directed to execute different procedures according to the number and type of arguments supplied by the caller.

The selection of which procedure to execute is made by the compiler from a list of alternative procedure names listed in an "interface" block. Each alternative procedure name is preceded by **module procedure** keywords to denote it is a "subprogram".

The interface block begins with the **interface** keyword, followed by the fundamental procedure name, and must be terminated by an **end interface** statement, with this syntax:

```
interface fundamental-procedure-name
    module procedure alternative-procedure-name
    module procedure alternative-procedure-name
    ...
end program
```

overload.f90

1 Begin a program that will use a module to output values
```
program main
    use output_module
    implicit none
```

2 Next, add calls to a module procedure that pass differing number and type of arguments
```
        call output(5)
        call output(4, 8, 16)
        call output(3.14)
end program
```

3 Now, save the file as **overload.f90**

4 Begin a module that declares a procedure with global scope

```fortran
module output_module
    implicit none
    public :: output
```

output.f90

5 Next, provide options to overload the declared procedure

```fortran
    interface output
        module procedure output_int
        module procedure output_ints
        module procedure output_real
    end interface
```

6 Now, define each of the option procedures

```fortran
    contains

    subroutine output_int(x)
        integer, intent(in) :: x
        write(*, '(/,A16,I4)' ) 'Integer value:', x
    end subroutine

    subroutine output_ints(x, y, z)
        integer, intent(in) :: x, y, z
        write(*, '(A16,3I4)' ) 'Integer values:', x, y, z
    end subroutine

    subroutine output_real(x)
        real, intent(in) :: x
        write(*, '(A16,F8.3)' ) 'Real value:', x
    end subroutine

end module
```

7 Save the file as **output.f90** then compile and run the program to see output from an overloaded procedure

```
Intel(r) oneAPI                    ×    +  ∨           —   □   ×

C:\MyPrograms>ifx /nologo overload.f90 output.f90

C:\MyPrograms>overload

  Integer value:    5
Integer values:    4   8  16
    Real value:    3.140

C:\MyPrograms>
```

Abstracting classes

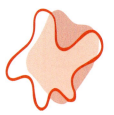

Fortran supports the concept of "abstract classes", in which an **abstract interface** specifies a set of procedures. This is useful to create flexible reusable code structures.

An abstract class is declared with the **abstract** keyword and lists its procedures using the **deferred** keyword, to denote their implementation will be defined later.

The **abstract interface** provides the procedure definitions, specifying their names and argument types but also does not supply the actual implementation. Instead, they include an **import** statement to provide a reference to the abstract class. A **contains** section can then include the actual procedure implementations.

model.f90

1 Begin a module by declaring an abstract class with two deferred procedures
```fortran
module class_Model
  implicit none
  type, abstract :: Model
    contains
      procedure(get_area), deferred :: area
      procedure(get_edge), deferred :: edge
  end type
```

2 Next, create a derived class to allow specific implementation of the deferred procedures
```fortran
  type, extends(Model) :: Rect
    contains
      procedure :: area
      procedure :: edge
  end type
```

3 Now, provide an interface block to define procedures and provide a reference to the abstract class
```fortran
  abstract interface
    function get_area(this, w, h)
      import Model
      class(Model) :: this
  end function

    function get_edge(this, w, h)
      import Model
      class(Model) :: this
    end function
  end interface
```

...cont'd

4 Finally, provide the actual procedure implementations
```
contains
function area(this, w, h) result(res)
    class(Rect) :: this
    real :: w, h, res
    res = w*h
end function

function edge(this, w, h) result(res)
    class(Rect) :: this
    real :: w, h, res
    res = (w*2) + (h*2)
end function
end module
```

5 Save the file as **model.f90** then begin a program that will use the module to output values
```
program main
    use class_Model
    implicit none
```

abstract.f90

6 Next, declare two variables and create a class instance
```
real :: w, h
type(Rect) :: square
```

7 Now, request user input then output calculated values
```
write(*, '(/,A13)', advance='no') 'Enter width: '
read(*,*) w
write(*, '(A13)', advance='no') 'Enter height: '
read(*,*) h
write(*, '(/,A5,7X,F5.2)' ) 'Area:', square%area(w, h)
write(*, '(A10,2X,F5.2)' ) 'Perimeter:', square%edge(w, h)
end program
```

8 Save the file as **abstract.f90** then compile and run the program, input values and see the output

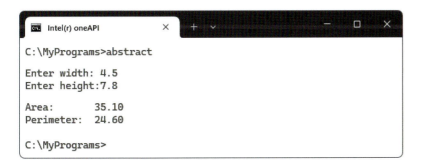

```
C:\MyPrograms>abstract

Enter width: 4.5
Enter height:7.8

Area:       35.10
Perimeter:  24.60

C:\MyPrograms>
```

151

Summary

- Real world objects have properties and behaviors that can be represented in Object Oriented Programming (OOP).

- Variables can store object properties, and procedures can emulate object behaviors in OOP.

- Variables and procedures contained within a class are known as its members, and procedures are known as its methods.

- Access to class members from outside the class is controlled by access specifiers in the class declaration.

- Setter and getter methods are used to store and retrieve data from class variable members.

- Setter and getter method definitions must receive a reference to the base type by including a **this** identifier argument.

- Class members are addressed by stating the class name followed by the **%** symbol and the member name.

- Class variable declarations can include the **optional** keyword and a default value be defined using the **present()** function.

- A derived class inherits members of the parent (base) class from which it is derived, in addition to its own members.

- Methods defined in a base class type and derived class type can redirect calls using the **=>** pointer association operator.

- An interface block can direct method calls to different procedures according to the number and type of arguments.

- The interface block can list procedure names preceded by **module procedure** keywords to denote each is a subprogram.

- An **abstract interface** provides procedure definitions as name and argument types but does not supply the implementation.

- An **abstract interface** can include an **import** statement to provide a reference to the abstract base class.

- A **contains** section can include the actual procedure implementations for an abstract class.

10 Threading apps

This chapter demonstrates parallel programming with Fortran coarrays.

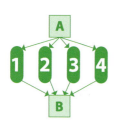

Calling images

Parallel computing allows multiple processes to be carried out simultaneously in individual threads. It is widely used in high-performance computing to improve speed and efficiency.

Fortran provides a Single Program Multiple Data (SPMD) approach to parallel computing with intrinsic support for "coarrays". Applications that use coarrays execute a program with multiple concurrent threads that Fortran refers to as "images". Coarray variables can be shared across the images using special constructs in a Partitioned Global Address Space (PGAS).

Most modern Intel CPUs support coarrays when used with the Intel ifx compiler. When compiling a program for coarrays, the compiler command must, however, include a **/Qcoarray** switch. This switch enables the coarray syntax for parallel programming and sets the relationship between the coarray images:

> ifx /Qcoarray *parallel-program.f90*

A coarray is declared in a Fortran program using the **codimension** keyword followed by **[ ]** square brackets containing an * asterisk character. The asterisk denotes that the coarray is distributed across all available images. This means that the coarray can be accessed by any image, and each image will have its own local part of the coarray. A declaration of an integer coarray looks like this:

> integer, codimension[*] :: *coarray-name*

Just as elements in a regular array can be referenced by their index number, each image in a coarray can be referenced by its index number. For example, to address the first image in a coarray and assign a value to it:

> *coarray-name*(1) = *value*

Additionally, an intrinsic **this_image()** function can be used to identify an individual image that is executing code by returning that image's index number.

A program using coarrays will run each image in parallel until completion but the images will not usually complete in the same order each time the program runs.

1 Begin a program that declares an integer coarray that can be accessed by any image in the parallel program

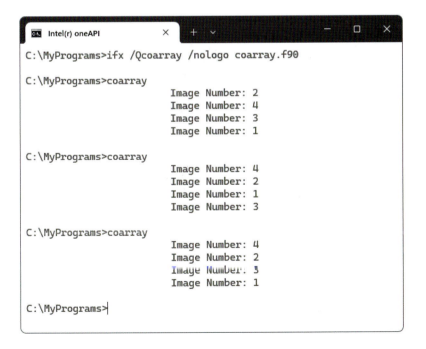

coarray.f90

```
program main
    implicit none
    integer(kind=1), codimension[*] :: coarray
```

2 Next, assign the index number of the current image to the coarray

```
coarray = this_image()
```

3 Now, output the index number of the current image

```
write(*, '(24X,A14,I2)' ) 'Image Number:', coarray
```

4 Save the file as **coarray.f90** then compile the program with this command

ifx /Qcoarray /nologo coarray.f90

5 Then, run the program repeatedly to see each image index number output – but notice that the images complete their execution in a different order each time

```
Intel(r) oneAPI

C:\MyPrograms>ifx /Qcoarray /nologo coarray.f90

C:\MyPrograms>coarray
                        Image Number: 2
                        Image Number: 4
                        Image Number: 3
                        Image Number: 1

C:\MyPrograms>coarray
                        Image Number: 4
                        Image Number: 2
                        Image Number: 1
                        Image Number: 3

C:\MyPrograms>coarray
                        Image Number: 4
                        Image Number: 2
                        Image Number: 3
                        Image Number: 1

C:\MyPrograms>
```

Syncing images

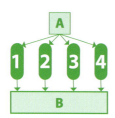

The default number of coarray images provided is determined by the runtime environment and is typically four images. The number of images can, however, be specified by a **/Qcoarray-num-images=** compiler switch. For example, to provide six images:

```
ifx /Qcoarray /Qcoarray-num-images=6 parallel-program.f90
```

The number of images available to the program can be revealed by calling an intrinsic **num_images()** function.

A program using coarrays will run each image in parallel until completion but the images will not, by default, reach the same point in the program before proceeding. This undesirable situation can be avoided by imposing discipline with a **sync all** statement. These keywords ensure synchronization so that all images will reach the same point before proceeding further.

sync.f90

1. Begin a program that declares a integer coarray and an integer variable
```fortran
program main
    implicit none
    integer(kind=1), codimension[*] :: coarray
    integer(kind=1) :: n
```

2. Next, initialize the coarray and variable with the current image index number and the total number of images
```fortran
coarray = this_image()
n = num_images()
```

3. Now, output the current image index and total
```fortran
write(*,'(A,I2,A3,I2)' ) &
    'HELLO from image', coarray, 'of', n
```

4. Then, add a "placeholder" comment
```fortran
! Synchronization to be added here.
```

5. Finally, output the current image index and total
```fortran
write(*,'(A,I2,A3,I2)' ) &
    'GOODBYE from image', coarray, 'of', n
```

6. Save the program as **sync.f90** then compile the program for six images and run the program to see the output
```
ifx /Qcoarray /Qcoarray-num-images=6 sync.f90
```

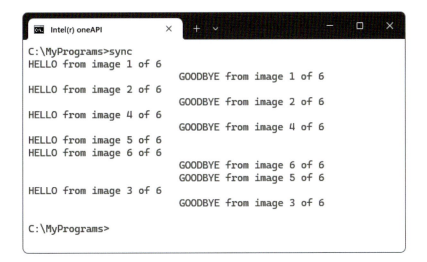

```
C:\MyPrograms>sync
HELLO from image 1 of 6
                        GOODBYE from image 1 of 6
HELLO from image 2 of 6
                        GOODBYE from image 2 of 6
HELLO from image 4 of 6
                        GOODBYE from image 4 of 6
HELLO from image 5 of 6
HELLO from image 6 of 6
                        GOODBYE from image 6 of 6
                        GOODBYE from image 5 of 6
HELLO from image 3 of 6
                        GOODBYE from image 3 of 6

C:\MyPrograms>
```

7 Notice how the images may proceed to execute their second output statement before other images complete their first

8 Replace the placeholder comment with a statement to resolve the undesirable situation

> sync all

9 Save the updated file then compile and run the program to see all images reach the same point before proceeding

```
C:\MyPrograms>sync
HELLO from image 2 of 6
HELLO from image 6 of 6
HELLO from image 5 of 6
HELLO from image 1 of 6
HELLO from image 4 of 6
HELLO from image 3 of 6
                        GOODBYE from image 2 of 6
                        GOODBYE from image 5 of 6
                        GOODBYE from image 3 of 6
                        GOODBYE from image 1 of 6
                        GOODBYE from image 6 of 6
                        GOODBYE from image 4 of 6

C:\MyPrograms>
```

Scanning images

Coarray images run as individual processes but it is important to recognize that changes made to coarray images are only implemented with synchronization. For example, the assignment in this coarray is only made to all images after synchronization, so the result may not be as expected if left unsynchronized:

```
C:\MyPrograms>type unsync.f90

program main
    implicit none
    integer(kind=1), codimension[*] :: coarray
    if (this_image() == 1) then
        coarray[1]  = 42
    end if
    print *, coarray[1]
end program

C:\MyPrograms>unsync
           0
           0
          42
          42

C:\MyPrograms>
```

The solution is to insert a **sync all** statement before calling the **print** function to ensure changes get made to all images before output:

```
if (this_image() == 1) then
    coarray[1] = 42
end if
sync all
print *, coarray[1]                    ! Outputs 42 42 42 42
```

When using coarrays it is typical to have all images perform processing tasks but have only one image perform output. Generally, the first image is used for output by testing if that is the current image, after first synchronizing all images:

```
sync all
if ( this_image() == 1 ) then
    write-output
end if
```

After synchronizing all images, a loop can usefully "scan" the value of all coarray images to perform calculations with their values.

1 Begin a program that declares an integer coarray and an integer variable

scan.f90

```fortran
program main
    implicit none
    integer(kind=1), codimension[*] :: coarr
    integer(kind=1) :: i
```

2 Next, initialize the coarray with the current image index number and synchronize all coarray values

```fortran
    coarr = this_image()
    sync all
```

3 Now, use the coarray values to calculate and output the Fibonacci sequence of numbers

```fortran
    if (this_image() == 1 ) then
        write(*, '(/,A)' ) 'Fibonacci Sequence...'
        do i = 1, 10
            if ( i > 2 ) then
                coarr[i] = coarr[i-1] + coarr[i-2]
            end if
            write(*, '(A5,I3,1X,A3,I5)' ) & 'Step', i, 'is', coarr[i]
        end do
    end if
end program
```

4 Save the file as **scan.f90** then compile the file with 10 coarray images and run the program to see the output

```
 Intel(r) oneAPI        ×    +  ∨              —   □   ×

C:\MyPrograms>ifx /Qcoarray /Qcoarray-num-images=10 scan.f90

C:\MyPrograms>scan

Fibonacci Sequence...
 Step  1  is     1
 Step  2  is     2
 Step  3  is     3
 Step  4  is     5
 Step  5  is     8
 Step  6  is    13
 Step  7  is    21
 Step  8  is    34
 Step  9  is    55
 Step 10  is    89

C:\MyPrograms>
```

Computing arrays

The previous coarray examples have all featured coarrays of single numbers ("scalar" values), but it is possible to have coarrays of regular arrays.

The declaration of a coarray of regular arrays defines the array data type and number of elements, then adds the **codimension** attribute and assigns an identifier name, with this syntax:

data-type, **dimension**(*size*), **codimension**[*] :: *coarray-name*

In effect, the regular arrays are distributed across different images.

lotto.f90

1 Begin a program that declares a coarray of regular arrays – with six elements in each regular array
```
program main
    implicit none
    integer (kind=1), dimension(6), codimension[*] :: coarr
```

2 Next, declare a real variable to store a random number, plus two integer variables and a logical variable
```
real(kind=4) :: rnd
integer(kind=1) :: i, j
logical :: unique
```

3 Now, call the intrinsic function to seed the random number generator to prevent repeat sequences
```
call random_seed()
```

4 Add a nested loop to assign a random number (1-59) to each element, initialize the logical variable, and include a placeholder comment
```
do i = 1, size(coarr)
    do while(.true.)
        call random_number(rnd)
        rnd = int(ceiling(rnd*59) )
        unique = .true.

        ! Uniqueness test to be added here.

    end do
    coarr(i) = rnd
end do
```

5 Replace the placeholder comment with a nested loop to ensure no numbers in the array elements are duplicated

```fortran
do j = 1, i-1
    if (coarr(j) == rnd) then
        unique = .false.
        exit
    end if
end do
if (unique) then
    exit
end if
```

6 Then, after the block of nested loops, output a heading

```fortran
if (this_image() == 1) then
    write(*, '(/,A,/)' ) 'Lotto Selections (1-59):'
end if
```

7 Finally, synchronize all coarray images and output the element values of each regular array

```fortran
sync all
print '(A,6I6)', 'Lucky Numbers:', coarr
end program
```

8 Save the file as **lotto.f90** then compile and run the program repeatedly to see different random selections

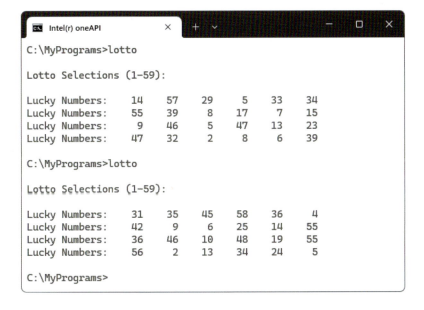

Here, the four groups of six random numbers are in the range 1 to 59 – to play the UK Lotto game or the US New York Lotto game.

Computing matrices

The previous coarray example features a coarray of one-dimensional arrays, but coarrays can have multi-dimensional arrays.

The declaration of a coarray of multi-dimensional arrays defines the array data type and number of elements in each dimension, then adds the **codimension** attribute and assigns an identifier name. A declaration with two-dimensional arrays has this syntax:

> *data-type*, **dimension**(*size,size*), **codimension**[*] :: *coarray-name*

The multi-dimensional arrays are distributed across different images. As coarray variables can be shared across the images using PGAS, the values can be collated to produce the sum of corresponding elements.

collate.f90

1 Begin a program that declares a two-dimensional integer matrix, plus two regular variables

```fortran
program main
    implicit none
    integer(kind=1), dimension(4,3), codimension[*] :: coarr
    integer(kind=1) :: i, j
```

2 Next, add nested loops to initialize all four elements of the first two columns of the matrix, then synchronize the images

```fortran
do i = 1, 4
    do j = 1, 2
        coarray(i, j) = this_image() + i + j
    end do
end do
sync all
```

3 Then, synchronize the images

```fortran
sync all
```

4 Now, add a loop to initialize all four elements of the third column of the matrix with the sum of the corresponding elements in the first two columns

```fortran
do i = 1, 4
    coarray(i, 3) = coarray(i, 1) + coarray(i, 2)
end do
```

5 Then, synchronize the images once more

```
sync all
```

6 Finally, output the values in all matrix elements of each coarray image

```
if (this_image() == 1) then
    do i = 1, num_images()
        write(*, '(/,A,I0)' ) 'Matrix from Image No.', i
        write(*, '(7X,4I8)' ) coarray(1:4,1)[i]
        write(*, '(7X,4I8)' ) coarray(1:4,2)[i]
        write(*, '(A7,4I8,/,A)' ), 'Totals:', &
            coarray(1:4,3)[i], repeat('-', 40)
    end do
end if
end program
```

7 Save the file as **collate.f90** then compile and run the program to see the output of collated values

```
Intel(r) oneAPI                    ×    +  ∨          —   □   ×

C:\MyPrograms>collate

Matrix from Image No.1
            3       4       5       6
            4       5       6       7
Totals:     7       9      11      13
----------------------------------------


Matrix from Image No.2
            4       5       6       7
            5       6       7       8
Totals:     9      11      13      15
----------------------------------------


Matrix from Image No.3
            5       6       7       8
            6       7       8       9
Totals:    11      13      15      17
----------------------------------------


Matrix from Image No.4
            6       7       8       9
            7       8       9      10
Totals:    13      15      17      19
----------------------------------------

C:\MyPrograms>
```

Using co_ intrinsics

Fortran provides several built-in "co_" intrinsic subroutines that perform collective operations on coarrays, such as finding maximum, minimum, and sum values of elements in each image:

- co_max(*result-coarray-name*, result_image=*image-number*)

- co_min(*result-coarray-name*, result_image=*image-number*)

- co_sum(*result-coarray-name*, result_image=*image-number*)

The coarray to be examined is assigned to a result-coarray of the same shape, then the result-coarray name is specified as the first argument to the function.

A valid image index number must then be assigned to the second argument to allow that image to reveal the results in output.

co_func.f90

1 Begin a program that declares four coarrays, plus three variables and a constant

```fortran
program main
    implicit none
    integer(kind=4), dimension(4), codimension[*] :: &
        coarr, maxi, mini, total
    real(kind=4) :: rnd
    integer(kind=1) :: i, num
    character(len=3), parameter :: S = '---'
```

2 Next, seed the random number generator and initialize the first coarray with random numbers (1-60)

```fortran
    call random_seed()
    do i = 1, size(coarr)
        call random_number(rnd)
        num = int(ceiling(rnd*59) )
        coarr(i) = num
    end do
```

3 Synchronize the coarray images and output their values

```fortran
    sync all
    print *, coarr
```

4 Now, initialize the other three coarrays with the values of the first coarray, replicating that coarray's images

```fortran
    maxi = coarr
    mini = coarr
    total= coarr
```

...cont'd

5 Then, examine each replicated coarray and allow image index 1 to reveal maximum, minimum, and sum results

```
call co_max(maxi, result_image=1)
call co_min(mini, result_image=1)
call co_sum(total, result_image=1)
```

6 Finally, output the results returned by the co_intrinsic functions

```
if (this_image()==1) then
    write(*, '(4(9X,A3))' ) S,S,S,S
    write(*, '(A4,I8,3I12)' ) 'Sum:', total
    write(*, '(4(9X,A3))' ) S,S,S,S
    write(*, '(A8,I4,3I12)' ) 'Maximum:', maxi
    write(*, '(A8,I4,3I12)' ) 'Minimum:', mini
    write(*, '(A)' ) repeat('_', 50)
end if
end program
```

7 Save the file as **co_func.f90** then compile and run the program to see the results from co_intrinsic functions

Reducing coarrays

Fortran provides a **co_reduce()** intrinsic subroutine that can be used to calculate the product of all elements in each coarray image. This function has an unusual syntax that requires three arguments to specify the coarray name, the name of a custom function to perform the operation, and an image index number to allow that image to reveal the results in output:

co_reduce(*coarray*, operation=*function*, result_image=*index*)

The specified custom function definition must begin with the **pure** keyword to denote that the function does not modify any global variables or perform any input/output operations – so it is safe to call in parallel computations. A custom function to calculate the product of all elements in each coarray image must be passed two arguments in order to multiply all element values.

co_reduce.f90

1 Begin a program that declares a coarray, plus three variables and a constant

```fortran
program main
    implicit none
    integer(kind=4), dimension(4), codimension[*] :: coarr
    real(kind=4) :: rnd
    integer(kind=1) :: i, num
    character(len=3), parameter :: S = '---'
```

2 Next, seed the random number generator and initialize the coarray with random numbers (1-10)

```fortran
    call random_seed()
    do i = 1, size(coarr)
        call random_number(rnd)
        num = int(ceiling(rnd*9) )
        coarr(i) = num
    end do
```

3 Synchronize the coarray images and output their values

```fortran
    sync all
    print *, coarr
```

4 Now, add a statement to specify the name of a custom function that will calculate the product of each coarray image and return the results to the first image

```fortran
    call co_reduce( coarr, &
        operation=get_product, result_image=1 )
```

5 Output the results that will be returned to the first image by the custom function

```
if (this_image() == 1) then
    write(*, '(4(9X,A3))' ) S,S,S,S
    write(*, '(A8,I4,3I12)' ) 'Product:', coarr
    write(*, '(4(9X,A3))' ) S,S,S,S
end if
```

6 Finally, add a contains section that defines the custom function to perform the required operation

```
contains
pure function get_product(a, b) result(res)
    integer(kind=4), intent(in) :: a, b
    integer(kind=4) :: res
    res = a * b
end function
end program
```

7 Save the file as **co_reduce.f90** then compile and run the program to see the results from the **co_reduce** subroutine

```
C:\ Intel(r) oneAPI                ×    +  ∨              —   □   ×

C:\MyPrograms>co_reduce
         8          1          3          8
         4          5          3          2
         3          6          2          7
         5          8          5          4
       ---        ---        ---        ---
Product: 480        240         90        448
       ---        ---        ---        ---


C:\MyPrograms>co_reduce
         4          5          3          2
         8          1          3          8
         2          2          7          8
         6          7          7          4
       ---        ---        ---        ---
Product: 384         70        441        512
       ---        ---        ---        ---

C:\MyPrograms>
```

Broadcasting values

Fortran provides a **co_broadcast()** intrinsic subroutine that can be used to set the element values of all coarray images from the element values in one particular image, with this syntax:

co_broadcast(*coarray-name*, source_image=*index-number*)

The call to the **co_broadcast()** subroutine acts as an assignment, so no explicit synchronization is required after the call.

broadcast.f90

1 Begin a program that declares a coarray, plus three variables
```fortran
program main
   implicit none
   integer(kind=1), dimension(4), codimension[*] :: coarr
   integer(kind=1) :: i, num
   real(kind=4) :: rnd
```

2 Next, seed the random number generator and initialize the coarray with random numbers (1-10)
```fortran
   call random_seed()
   do i = 1, size(coarr)
      call random_number(rnd)
      num = int(ceiling(rnd*9) )
      coarr(i) = num
   end do
```

3 Synchronize the coarray images and output their values
```fortran
   write(*, '(A,I2,A2,4I4)' ) 'Image', this_image(), ':', coarr
   sync all
```

4 Now, output a separation line
```fortran
   if (this_image() == 1) write(*, '(A)' ) repeat('-', 40)
```

5 Then, assign all values from "Image 4" to all images
```fortran
   call co_broadcast(coarr, source_image=4)
```

6 Output their new values and synchronize the coarray images
```fortran
   write(*, '(A,I2,A2,4I4)' ) 'Image', this_image(), ':', coarr
   sync all
```

7 Then, assign new values to "Image 1", and output the values of that image within separation lines

```
if (this_image() == 1) then
    coarr(1:4) = [10, 20, 30, 40]
    write(*, '(A)' ) repeat('-', 40)
    write(*, '(A,I2,A2,4I4)' ) 'Image', this_image(), ':', coarr
    write(*, '(A)' ) repeat('-', 40)
end if
```

8 Assign all new values from "Image 1" to all images

```
call co_broadcast(coarr, source_image=1)
```

9 Output the new values and synchronize the coarray images once more

```
write(*, '(A,I2,A2,4I4)' ) 'Image', this_image(), ':', coarr
sync all
```

10 Save the file as **broadcast.f90** then compile and run the program to see the broadcast values

```
C:\MyPrograms>broadcast
Image 2 :    8    3    8    7
Image 4 :    4    7    8    2
Image 3 :    6    5    8    4
Image 1 :    4    2    4    7
----------------------------------------
Image 4 :    4    7    8    2
Image 2 :    4    7    8    2
Image 3 :    4    7    8    2
Image 1 :    4    7    8    2
----------------------------------------
Image 1 :   10   20   30   40
----------------------------------------
Image 1 :   10   20   30   40
Image 4 :   10   20   30   40
Image 3 :   10   20   30   40
Image 2 :   10   20   30   40

C:\MyPrograms>
```

Summary

- Parallel computing allows multiple processes to be carried out simultaneously in individual threads.

- Coarrays execute a program with multiple concurrent images.

- Coarray variables can be shared across images using special constructs in a Partitioned Global Address Space (PGAS).

- When compiling a program for coarrays, the ifx compiler command must include a **/Qcoarray** switch.

- A coarray declaration uses the **codimension** keyword followed by [ ] square brackets containing an * asterisk character.

- Each image in a coarray can be referenced by its index number.

- The intrinsic **this_image()** function returns the index number of the image that is currently executing code.

- The ifx compiler command may specify the number of images to create using a **/Qcoarray-num-images=** compiler switch.

- Images will not reach the same point in the program before proceeding unless a **sync_all** statement is added.

- Changes made to coarray images are only implemented with synchronization.

- Generally, the first image is used for output by testing if that is the current image, after first synchronizing all images.

- Coarrays may comprise single numbers, regular flat arrays, or multi-dimensional arrays.

- Fortran provides several intrinsic subroutines that perform collective operations on coarrays.

- The **co_max**, **co_min**, and **co_sum** subroutines return the maximum, minimum, and sum of elements in each image.

- The **co_reduce()** subroutine can be used to calculate the product of all elements in each coarray image.

- The **co_broadcast()** subroutine can be used to set the element values of images from the element values in one image.

11 Analyzing data

This chapter demonstrates how Fortran can be used to import, clean, and analyze data to gain insights.

Loading data

Modern Fortran has become increasingly popular to process the large amounts of data gathered by devices in today's world, largely due to its ability to deal with arrays efficiently.

Datasets are often established as lists of comma-separated values in CSV file format, and these can be imported into two-dimensional Fortran arrays for analysis. The datasets can be huge but for the purpose of demonstration, a compact dataset is used throughout this chapter. This features the names of several plug-in hybrid vehicles (PHEV) together with some of their properties:

phev-data.csv

	A	B	C	D	E	F	G	H
1	MAKE	MODEL	ENGINE	MPG	E-RANGE	CARGO	0-60MPH	$BASE
2	Ford	Escape	2.5	101	37	34.4	7.7	40500
3	Lexus	RX450h	2.5	36	37	29.6	6.2	68730
4	Toyota	RAV4P	2.5	94	42	34	5.5	43440
5	Lexus	NX450h	2.5	85	37	22.7	5.6	58755
6	Kia	Sportage	1.6	84	34	34.5	7.1	40695
7	Volvo	XC90	2	58	42	5	5	71900
8	Hyundai	Tucson	1.6	80	33	31.9	7.1	38475
9	Kia	Sorento	1.6	79	32	13	7.4	49940
10	Alfa	Tonale	1.3	77	33	22.9	5.7	44940
11	Volvo	XC60	2	63	36	8	4.3	57900
12	BMW	X5	3	?	39	34	4.6	72500
13	Audi	Q5	2	60	23	25.9	5.9	59590
14	Mazda	CX-90	2.5	56	26	14.9	6.2	47445
15	Rover	Autobio	3	?	51	?	4.7	118200
16	Jeep	Wrangler	2	49	22	28	6.8	50695
17	Porsche	Cayenne	3	?	51	22	3.5	91700
18	Bentley	Bentayga	3	47	25	16.9	5.2	203200
19	BMW	XM	4.4	46	31	18.6	4.1	159000

phev.f90

1 Begin a program that declares two 2D arrays to hold data and two variables to keep track of their shape

```fortran
program main
    implicit none
    character(len=9), dimension(:,:), allocatable :: table, proxy
    integer(kind=1) :: num_cols, num_rows

    ! Statements to be inserted here.

end program
```

2 Insert statements to load data and display a confirmation

```fortran
    call load_data()
    call display('PHEV Data Loaded')
```

3 Next, begin a **contains** section to contain the procedures

```
contains

    ! Procedures to be inserted here.
```

4 Now, begin a procedure that declares a constant and variables to implement data importation

```
subroutine load_data()
    character(len=16), parameter :: file_name = 'phev-data.csv'
    character(len=480) :: line
    integer(kind=1) :: unit_num, ios, i
```

5 Ensure the CSV file exists, or report an error

```
    open(newunit=unit_num, file=file_name, &
        status='old', iostat=ios)
    if (ios /= 0) then
        write(0, '(/,A,I2)' ) 'Error: File not found. IOSTAT=', ios
        stop
    end if
```

6 Count the number of columns in the CSV file

```
    read(unit_num,'(A)') line
    num_cols = 1
    do i = 1, len_trim(line)
        if (line(i:i) == ',') num_cols = num_cols + 1
    end do
    rewind(unit_num)
```

7 Then, count the number of rows in the CSV file

```
    num_rows = 0
    do
        read(unit_num, '(A)', iostat=ios) line
        if (ios /= 0) exit
        num_rows = num_rows + 1
    end do
    rewind(unit_num)
```

8 Shape the table matrix to match the shape of the CSV file

```
    allocate(table(num_cols,num_rows))
```

9 Finally, load all CSV data into the table matrix

```
    read(unit_num, fmt=*, iostat=ios) table
    if (ios /= 0) close(unit_num)
end subroutine
```

continues on next page

Displaying data

10 Insert a procedure to output all data from the table matrix

```
subroutine display(str)
    character(len=*) :: str
    integer(kind=1) :: i
    print '(/,2A)', str, repeat('.',10)
    do i = 1, num_rows
        print *, table(:num_cols,i)
    end do
    print *, repeat('-',60)
end subroutine
```

11 Compile and run the program to see the loaded data

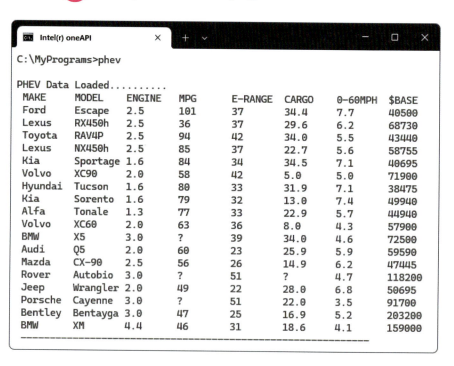

```
Intel(r) oneAPI                                    —  □  ✕

C:\MyPrograms>phev

PHEV Data Loaded..........
MAKE      MODEL     ENGINE   MPG    E-RANGE   CARGO   0-60MPH   $BASE
Ford      Escape    2.5      101    37        34.4    7.7       40500
Lexus     RX450h    2.5      36     37        29.6    6.2       68730
Toyota    RAV4P     2.5      94     42        34.0    5.5       43440
Lexus     NX450h    2.5      85     37        22.7    5.6       58755
Kia       Sportage  1.6      84     34        34.5    7.1       40695
Volvo     XC90      2.0      58     42        5.0     5.0       71900
Hyundai   Tucson    1.6      80     33        31.9    7.1       38475
Kia       Sorento   1.6      79     32        13.0    7.4       49940
Alfa      Tonale    1.3      77     33        22.9    5.7       44940
Volvo     XC60      2.0      63     36        8.0     4.3       57900
BMW       X5        3.0      ?      39        34.0    4.6       72500
Audi      Q5        2.0      60     23        25.9    5.9       59590
Mazda     CX-90     2.5      56     26        14.9    6.2       47445
Rover     Autobio   3.0      ?      51        ?       4.7       118200
Jeep      Wrangler  2.0      49     22        28.0    6.8       50695
Porsche   Cayenne   3.0      ?      51        22.0    3.5       91700
Bentley   Bentayga  3.0      47     25        16.9    5.2       203200
BMW       XM        4.4      46     31        18.6    4.1       159000
_____
```

The data can be cleaned by subsequent procedures in the following ways:

- Remove columns not relevant for a proposed comparison.

- Remove rows not relevant for a proposed comparison.

- Remove rows with empty cells (denoted here by ? characters).

- Remove rows with values outside a desired range.

Replicating data

The technique to remove an unwanted row or column from a matrix is a three-step process that first requires all table matrix data to be copied into a proxy matrix of the same shape:

The next step requires the table matrix to be reshaped by removing a row or column:

Finally, the data can be copied back from the proxy matrix into the table matrix – except the row or column to be removed:

It is useful, therefore, to create a utility procedure to populate the proxy matrix with all data currently held in the table matrix.

① Insert a procedure in the **contains** section to shape the proxy matrix to match the shape of the table matrix, and to then copy all data to the proxy matrix

```
subroutine clone()
   integer(kind=1) :: i, j
   allocate(proxy(num_cols,num_rows))
   do i = 1, num_rows
      do j = 1, num_cols
         proxy(:,i) = table(:,i)
      end do
   end do
end subroutine
```

continues on next page

Removing columns

The identity of a column to be removed from a matrix can be established by getting its index position in the column header row.

1 Insert a procedure in the **contains** section that accepts a column header argument and can store its index position

```
subroutine drop_col(col_hdr)
    character(len=*) :: col_hdr
    integer(kind=1) :: col_pos, i, j
```

2 Next, use the utility procedure created on page 175 to populate the proxy matrix

```
call clone()
```

3 Now, get the index position of the column header

```
col_pos = findloc(table(:,1), col_hdr, dim=1)
```

4 Reduce the number of columns in the tracking variable

```
num_cols = num_cols - 1
```

5 Then, reshape the table matrix to have one less column

```
deallocate(table)
allocate(table(num_cols,num_rows))
```

6 Copy all data from the proxy matrix back to the table matrix – except for the column to be removed

```
do i = 1, num_cols
    do j = 1, num_rows
        if (i >= col_pos) then
            table(i,j) = proxy(i+1,j)
        else
            table(i,j) = proxy(i,j)
        end if
    end do
end do
```

7 Finally, release the allocated proxy matrix memory

```
deallocate(proxy)
end subroutine
```

8 Insert statements in the main program section to remove a column and display a confirmation

```
call drop_col('ENGINE')
call display('Unwanted ENGINE  column removed')
```

9 Compile and run the program to see the specified column get removed

```
C:\MyPrograms>phev

PHEV Data Loaded..........
MAKE      MODEL     ENGINE  MPG    E-RANGE  CARGO   0-60MPH  $BASE
Ford      Escape    2.5     101    37       34.4    7.7      40500
Lexus     RX450h    2.5     36     37       29.6    6.2      68730
Toyota    RAV4P     2.5     94     42       34.0    5.5      43440
Lexus     NX450h    2.5     85     37       22.7    5.6      58755
Kia       Sportage  1.6     84     34       34.5    7.1      40695
Volvo     XC90      2.0     58     42       5.0     5.0      71900
Hyundai   Tucson    1.6     80     33       31.9    7.1      38475
Kia       Sorento   1.6     79     32       13.0    7.4      49940
Alfa      Tonale    1.3     77     33       22.9    5.7      44940
Volvo     XC60      2.0     63     36       8.0     4.3      57900
BMW       X5        3.0     ?      39       34.0    4.6      72500
Audi      Q5        2.0     60     23       25.9    5.9      59590
Mazda     CX-90     2.5     56     26       14.9    6.2      47445
Rover     Autobio   3.0     ?      51       ?       4.7      118200
Jeep      Wrangler  2.0     49     22       28.0    6.8      50695
Porsche   Cayenne   3.0     ?      51       22.0    3.5      91700
Bentley   Bentayga  3.0     47     25       16.9    5.2      203200
BMW       XM        4.4     46     31       18.6    4.1      159000
-----------------------------------------------------------------

Unwanted ENGINE column removed..........
MAKE      MODEL     MPG    E-RANGE  CARGO   0-60MPH  $BASE
Ford      Escape    101    37       34.4    7.7      40500
Lexus     RX450h    36     37       29.6    6.2      68730
Toyota    RAV4P     94     42       34.0    5.5      43440
Lexus     NX450h    85     37       22.7    5.6      58755
Kia       Sportage  84     34       34.5    7.1      40695
Volvo     XC90      58     42       5.0     5.0      71900
Hyundai   Tucson    80     33       31.9    7.1      38475
Kia       Sorento   79     32       13.0    7.4      49940
Alfa      Tonale    77     33       22.9    5.7      44940
Volvo     XC60      63     36       8.0     4.3      57900
BMW       X5        ?      39       34.0    4.6      72500
Audi      Q5        60     23       25.9    5.9      59590
Mazda     CX-90     56     26       14.9    6.2      47445
Rover     Autobio   ?      51       ?       4.7      118200
Jeep      Wrangler  49     22       28.0    6.8      50695
Porsche   Cayenne   ?      51       22.0    3.5      91700
Bentley   Bentayga  47     25       16.9    5.2      203200
BMW       XM        46     31       18.6    4.1      159000
-----------------------------------------------------------------
```

continues on next page

Removing rows

The identity of a row to be removed from a matrix can be established by getting its index position in the row header column.

1 Insert a procedure in the **contains** section that accepts row header text as its argument and begins by providing a variable to store its index position

```
subroutine drop_row(row_hdr)
   character(len=9), dimension(num_rows) :: row_hdrs
   integer(kind=1) :: row_pos, i, j
```

2 Next, populate the proxy matrix

```
call clone()
```

3 Now, get the index position of the row header

```
row_hdrs = reshape(table(:1,:),[num_rows])
row_pos = findloc(row_hdrs, row_hdr, dim=1)
```

4 Reduce the number of rows in the tracking variable

```
num_rows = num_rows - 1
```

5 Then, reshape the table matrix to have one less row

```
deallocate(table)
allocate(table(num_cols,num_rows))
```

6 Copy all data from the proxy matrix back to the table matrix – except for the row to be removed

```
do i = 1, num_rows
   if ( i >= row_pos) then
      table(:,i) = proxy(:,i+1)
   else
      table(:,i) = proxy(:,i)
   end if
end do
```

7 Finally, release the allocated proxy matrix memory

```
deallocate(proxy)
end subroutine
```

8 Insert statements in the main program section to remove two rows and display a confirmation

```
call drop_row('Audi')
call drop_row('Jeep')
call display('Unwanted Audi & Jeep rows removed')
```

9 Compile and run the program to see the specified rows get removed

```
Intel(r) oneAPI

Unwanted ENGINE column removed..........
MAKE     MODEL    MPG    E-RANGE   CARGO   0-60MPH   $BASE
Ford     Escape   101    37        34.4    7.7       40500
Lexus    RX450h   36     37        29.6    6.2       68730
Toyota   RAV4P    94     42        34.0    5.5       43440
Lexus    NX450h   85     37        22.7    5.6       58755
Kia      Sportage 84     34        34.5    7.1       40695
Volvo    XC90     58     42        5.0     5.0       71900
Hyundai  Tucson   80     33        31.9    7.1       38475
Kia      Sorento  79     32        13.0    7.4       49940
Alfa     Tonale   77     33        22.9    5.7       44940
Volvo    XC60     63     36        8.0     4.3       57900
BMW      X5       ?      39        34.0    4.6       72500
Audi     Q5       60     23        25.9    5.9       59590
Mazda    CX-90    56     26        14.9    6.2       47445
Rover    Autobio  ?      51        ?       4.7       118200
Jeep     Wrangler 49     22        28.0    6.8       50695
Porsche  Cayenne  ?      51        22.0    3.5       91700
Bentley  Bentayga 47     25        16.9    5.2       203200
BMW      XM       46     31        18.6    4.1       159000
------------------------------------------------------------

Unwanted Audi & Jeep rows removed..........
MAKE     MODEL    MPG    E-RANGE   CARGO   0-60MPH   $BASE
Ford     Escape   101    37        34.4    7.7       40500
Lexus    RX450h   36     37        29.6    6.2       68730
Toyota   RAV4P    94     42        34.0    5.5       43440
Lexus    NX450h   85     37        22.7    5.6       58755
Kia      Sportage 84     34        34.5    7.1       40695
Volvo    XC90     58     42        5.0     5.0       71900
Hyundai  Tucson   80     33        31.9    7.1       38475
Kia      Sorento  79     32        13.0    7.4       49940
Alfa     Tonale   77     33        22.9    5.7       44940
Volvo    XC60     63     36        8.0     4.3       57900
BMW      X5       ?      39        34.0    4.6       72500
Mazda    CX-90    56     26        14.9    6.2       47445
Rover    Autobio  ?      51        ?       4.7       118200
Porsche  Cayenne  ?      51        22.0    3.5       91700
Bentley  Bentayga 47     25        16.9    5.2       203200
BMW      XM       46     31        18.6    4.1       159000
------------------------------------------------------------
```

continues on next page

Removing empties

Rows containing invalid data, such as empty cells, can be identified as bad and removed using the procedure created on page 179.

1 Insert a procedure in the **contains** section that will assign the row header text of bad rows to an array

```
subroutine drop_bad()
    character(len=9), dimension(:), allocatable :: bad_rows
    character(len=9), dimension(num_cols) :: row
    character(len=9) :: cell
    integer(kind=4) :: num, ios, i, j, k
    logical :: is_valid
```

2 Next, populate the proxy matrix

```
call clone()
```

3 Now, identify rows that should only contain characters that appear in integer and real numbers

```
do i = 2, num_rows
    row = proxy(:,i)
    do j = 3, size(row)
        cell = row(j)
        do k = 1, len_trim(cell)
            is_valid = .true.
                if( index('1234567890.', cell(k:k)) == 0) then
                    is_valid = .false.
                end if
        end do
        if(.not. is_valid) then
            bad_rows = [bad_rows,row(1)]
            exit
        end if
    end do
end do
```

4 Then, release the allocated proxy matrix memory

```
deallocate(proxy)
```

5 Finally, remove all rows identified as bad

```
do i = 1, size(bad_rows)
    call drop_row(bad_rows(i))
end do
end subroutine
```

6 Insert statements in the main program section to remove bad rows and display a confirmation

```
call drop_bad()
call display('Invalid ? rows removed')
```

7 Compile and run the program to see bad rows removed

```
┌──────────────────────────────────────────────────────────────┐
│ ▣  Intel(r) oneAPI          ×   + ∨        —   □   ✕          │
├──────────────────────────────────────────────────────────────┤
Unwanted Audi & Jeep rows removed..........
MAKE      MODEL      MPG    E-RANGE   CARGO    0-60MPH   $BASE
Ford      Escape     101    37        34.4     7.7       40500
Lexus     RX450h     36     37        29.6     6.2       68730
Toyota    RAV4P      94     42        34.0     5.5       43440
Lexus     NX450h     85     37        22.7     5.6       58755
Kia       Sportage   84     34        34.5     7.1       40695
Volvo     XC90       58     42        5.0      5.0       71900
Hyundai   Tucson     80     33        31.9     7.1       38475
Kia       Sorento    79     32        13.0     7.4       49940
Alfa      Tonale     77     33        22.9     5.7       44940
Volvo     XC60       63     36        8.0      4.3       57900
BMW       X5         ?      39        34.0     4.6       72500
Mazda     CX-90      56     26        14.9     6.2       47445
Rover     Autobio    ?      51        ?        4.7       118200
Porsche   Cayenne    ?      51        22.0     3.5       91700
Bentley   Bentayga   47     25        16.9     5.2       203200
BMW       XM         46     31        18.6     4.1       159000
--------------------------------------------------------------

Invalid ? rows removed..........
MAKE      MODEL      MPG    E-RANGE   CARGO    0-60MPH   $BASE
Ford      Escape     101    37        34.4     7.7       40500
Lexus     RX450h     36     37        29.6     6.2       68730
Toyota    RAV4P      94     42        34.0     5.5       43440
Lexus     NX450h     85     37        22.7     5.6       58755
Kia       Sportage   84     34        34.5     7.1       40695
Volvo     XC90       58     42        5.0      5.0       71900
Hyundai   Tucson     80     33        31.9     7.1       38475
Kia       Sorento    79     32        13.0     7.4       49940
Alfa      Tonale     77     33        22.9     5.7       44940
Volvo     XC60       63     36        8.0      4.3       57900
Mazda     CX-90      56     26        14.9     6.2       47445
Bentley   Bentayga   47     25        16.9     5.2       203200
BMW       XM         46     31        18.6     4.1       159000
--------------------------------------------------------------
```

continues on next page

Removing out-of-range

Rows containing outlier data that is outside a desired range can also be identified as bad and removed using the procedure created on pages 178-179.

1 Insert a procedure in the **contains** section that will assign the row header text of bad rows to an array
```
subroutine drop_out_of_range()
    character(len=9), dimension(:), allocatable :: bad_rows
    character(len=9), dimension(num_cols) :: row
    integer(kind=4) :: num, ios, i, j
```

2 Next, populate the proxy matrix
```
call clone()
```

3 Now, identify rows that contain a base price above $60K
```
do i = 2, num_rows
    row = proxy(:,i)
    do j = num_cols, num_cols
        read( row(j), '(I6)', iostat=ios) num
            if(num > 60000 ) then
                bad_rows = [bad_rows,row(1)]
                exit
            end if
    end do
end do
```

4 Then, release the allocated proxy matrix memory
```
deallocate(proxy)
```

5 Finally, remove all rows identified as out-of-range
```
do i = 1, size(bad_rows)
    call drop_row(bad_rows(i))
end do
end subroutine
```

6 Insert statements in the main program section to remove out-of-range rows and display a confirmation
```
call drop_out_of_range()
call display('Out-of-range $60k+ rows removed')
```

7 Compile and run the program to see rows containing out-of-range values get removed

```
Intel(r) oneAPI              ×    + ∨              —   □   ✕

Invalid ? rows removed..........
  MAKE       MODEL      MPG     E-RANGE  CARGO    0-60MPH  $BASE
  Ford       Escape     101     37       34.4     7.7      40500
  Lexus      RX450h     36      37       29.6     6.2      68730
  Toyota     RAV4P      94      42       34.0     5.5      43440
  Lexus      NX450h     85      37       22.7     5.6      58755
  Kia        Sportage   84      34       34.5     7.1      40695
  Volvo      XC90       58      42       5.0      5.0      71900
  Hyundai    Tucson     80      33       31.9     7.1      38475
  Kia        Sorento    79      32       13.0     7.4      49940
  Alfa       Tonale     77      33       22.9     5.7      44940
  Volvo      XC60       63      36       8.0      4.3      57900
  Mazda      CX-90      56      26       14.9     6.2      47445
  Bentley    Bentayga   47      25       16.9     5.2      203200
  BMW        XM         46      31       18.6     4.1      159000
  -----------------------------------------------------------

Out-of-range $60k+ rows removed..........
  MAKE       MODEL      MPG     E-RANGE  CARGO    0-60MPH  $BASE
  Ford       Escape     101     37       34.4     7.7      40500
  Toyota     RAV4P      94      42       34.0     5.5      43440
  Lexus      NX450h     85      37       22.7     5.6      58755
  Kia        Sportage   84      34       34.5     7.1      40695
  Hyundai    Tucson     80      33       31.9     7.1      38475
  Kia        Sorento    79      32       13.0     7.4      49940
  Alfa       Tonale     77      33       22.9     5.7      44940
  Volvo      XC60       63      36       8.0      4.3      57900
  Mazda      CX-90      56      26       14.9     6.2      47445
  -----------------------------------------------------------
```

It is useful to create a utility procedure to calculate the best result of two compared fields to gain useful insights from data.

1 Insert a procedure in the **contains** section to accept an array of scores and return the index position of the best result

```fortran
function rate(score) result(best_index)
   real(kind=4), dimension(num_rows-1) :: score
   real(kind=4) :: best_score
   integer(kind=1) :: i, best_index
   best_score = score(1)
   best_index = 1
   do i = 1, size(score)
      if (score(i) > best_score) then
         best_score = score(i)
         best_index = i
      end if
   end do
end function
```

continues on next page

Gaining insights

Data within the various categories can be compared to recognize the optimum values and best benefits.

1 Insert a procedure in the **contains** section that will assign cells containing numeric values into real data type arrays

```
subroutine get_insights()
    real(kind=4), dimension(num_rows-1) :: &
        mpg, rng, cgo, mph, bas
    real(kind=4), dimension(num_rows-1) :: score
    integer(kind=1) :: i, ios, col_pos
    character(len=12), parameter :: line = '(A32,2X,2A8)'
```

2 Next, populate the real data type arrays

```
do i = 2, num_rows
    read( table(3:,i), *, iostat=ios) mpg(i-1)
    read( table(4:,i), *, iostat=ios) rng(i-1)
    read( table(5:,i), *, iostat=ios) cgo(i-1)
    read( table(6:,i), *, iostat=ios) mph(i-1)
    read( table(7:,i), *, iostat=ios) bas(i-1)
end do
```

3 Now, output the optimum values in each category

```
print '(/,2A)', 'Insights', repeat('.',10)
col_pos = 1+findloc(mpg, maxval(mpg), dim=1)
    print line, 'Best MPG: ', table(:2,col_pos)
col_pos = 1+findloc(rng, maxval(rng), dim=1)
    print line, 'Best E-Range: ', table(:2,col_pos)
col_pos = 1+findloc(cgo, maxval(cgo), dim=1)
    print line, 'Best Cargo: ', table(:2,col_pos)
col_pos = 1+findloc(mph, minval(mph), dim=1)
    print line, 'Quickest: ', table(:2,col_pos)
col_pos = 1+findloc(bas, minval(bas), dim=1)
    print line, 'Cheapest: ', table(:2,col_pos)
print *, repeat('-',60)
```

4 Then, use the utility function created on page 183 to calculate a score for each car and output the best benefit result

```
do i = 1, size(mpg)
    score(i) = mpg(i) / bas(i)
end do
print line, 'Best MPG/$:', table(:2,rate(score)+1)

do i = 1, size(rng)
    score(i) = rng(i) / bas(i)
end do
print line, 'Best E-Range/$:', table(:2,rate(score)+1)
```

```
          do i = 1, size(cgo)
              score(i) = cgo(i) / bas(i)
          end do
          print line, 'Best Cargo/$:', table(:2,rate(score)+1)

          do i = 1, size(mph)
              score(i) = (1.0/ mph(i) / bas(i) )
          end do
          print line, 'Best MPH/$:', table(:2,rate(score)+1)

          do i = 1, size(mph)
              score(i) = (1.0/ mph(i) / mpg(i) )
          end do
          print line, 'Best MPH/MPG:', table(:2,rate(score)+1)
      end subroutine
```

5 Insert a statement in the main program section to get insights then compile and run the program to see output

```
          call get_insights()
```

```
Intel(r) oneAPI                        ×   +  ∨              —  □  ×

Out-of-range $60k+ rows removed..........
MAKE      MODEL      MPG    E-RANGE  CARGO   0-60MPH  $BASE
Ford      Escape     101    37       34.4    7.7      40500
Toyota    RAV4P      94     42       34.0    5.5      43440
Lexus     NX450h     85     37       22.7    5.6      58755
Kia       Sportage   84     34       34.5    7.1      40695
Hyundai   Tucson     80     33       31.9    7.1      38475
Kia       Sorento    79     32       13.0    7.4      49940
Alfa      Tonale     77     33       22.9    5.7      44940
Volvo     XC60       63     36       8.0     4.3      57900
Mazda     CX-90      56     26       14.9    6.2      47445
------------------------------------------------------------

Insights..........
                   Best MPG:     Ford     Escape
                Best E-Range:    Toyota   RAV4P
                  Best Cargo:    Kia      Sportage
                   Quickest:     Volvo    XC60
                   Cheapest:     Hyundai  Tucson
------------------------------------------------------------
                 Best MPG/$:     Ford     Escape
              Best E-Range/$:    Toyota   RAV4P
                Best Cargo/$:    Ford     Escape
                 Best MPH/$:     Toyota   RAV4P
                Best MPH/MPG:    Volvo    XC60

C:\MyPrograms>
```

Summary

- Datasets are often established as lists of comma-separated values in CSV file format.

- CSV data can be imported into two-dimensional Fortran arrays for analysis.

- A table matrix can be shaped to match the shape of a CSV file by counting the number of rows and columns.

- Data can be cleaned by removing unwanted columns and by removing rows that are unwanted or invalid.

- Removal of rows or columns first requires all table matrix data to be copied into a proxy matrix of the same shape.

- A utility procedure can be created to populate a proxy matrix with all data currently held in a table matrix.

- A table matrix is reshaped by calling the **deallocate()** function then calling the **allocate()** function to specify the new shape.

- The reshaped table matrix can then be populated by copying the desired data from the proxy matrix.

- The identity of a column to be removed can be established by getting its index position in the column header row.

- The identity of a row to be removed can be established by getting its index position in the row header column.

- Rows containing empty cells or data that is outside a desired range can be seen as invalid and removed to clean the data.

- A utility procedure can be created to calculate the best result of two compared fields to gain useful insights from data.

- Data within the various categories of a table matrix can be compared to recognize the optimum values and best benefits.

Index

Q

R

S